The Gospel-Centered Church

A Study in the Book of Titus

By Daniel D Hughes

kerugma
press
kp

Kerugma Press
Gallup, New Mexico

The Gospel-Centered Church

Table of Contents

Acknowledgements

My study of the wonderful book of Titus has now covered over two years. The time I have spent in this book has been both challenging and deeply edifying. Dan Fredericks, thank you for your heart for the health of the local church and for putting together The Titus Template, which was the foundation for this book. I want to give a special thanks to Gary Knode for giving me the idea and inspiration for this book. I am also deeply indebted to those who have encouraged me along the way and to those who have taken the time to review and correct my many mistakes. Specifically I want to thank Jacob, Amy, Don and Scottie for all of their hard work and advice. I must also thank Doug Hughes, my father, for his constant encouragement and many good suggestions along the way. Most of all, I want to thank my wife Sarah, for the many, many hours spent pouring over the grammar and content of this book. I cannot imagine trying to do this (or anything else for that matter) without you! Thank you Sarah for your joyful patience with me and my work, even when it added to your already crazy schedule. You are all a reminder of God's overflowing grace, and for that may he receive the praise that he so richly deserves.

The Gospel-Centered Church

Introduction to This Study

So what is a gospel-centered church? Is this just another simple attempt at a trendy title, using a new catchword to attract a fad-driven Christian audience? To be honest, I do fear that the words gospel or gospel-centered are over used today, not because there is anything wrong with them, but because very good words can easily lose their meaning when they are over used (or maybe under explained). As people who drift towards excitement and movement, we are too easily captivated by words and phrases simply because we love the new and exciting and not for any real deep-seated commitment to the issue at hand. It is my earnest desire that each reader truly consider the implications of this title (which we will discuss briefly) and then prayerfully examine their personal understanding of how God intends to build his church. The Scripture is our one guide and the Holy Spirit is our ultimate teacher. May we seek to be faithful to the charge that we have been given and see local congregations that are centered on the message of the gospel.

What I mean by gospel-centered church is simply a local church where the people are genuinely converted by the gospel, fully captivated by the promise of the gospel and living in a way that adorns the gospel of Jesus Christ. The goal is not to encourage a vocabulary filled with the word "gospel," but rather to focus our attention on what Paul refers to as "sound doctrine." The church must be built on a solid understanding and application of these doctrines. This is why the book of Titus is so valuable to us. In it, we find short, simple and clear instructions on how to build up and establish a struggling local church. Nevertheless, I must warn you as the reader – this may fly in the face of the more modern, trendy wisdom that packs endless volumes of church growth books today. However, the goal is not to be controversial, but clear and faithful to what God has taken the time to give us in the Scriptures. If God has truly taken the time and effort to give us instructions, it is the least we can do to give those instructions absolute priority. Would it not be far better to spend a lifetime pouring over a few simple chapters that come directly from God than 5 minutes on what comes from man? One of the main goals of this work is simply to refocus our attention on what we may have unintentionally neglected in our search for answers.

In fact, the book of Titus is so short you may have overlooked it. It is only three chapters long and yet Martin Luther said, *"This is a short epistle, but it contains such a quintessence of Christian doctrine, and is composed in such a masterly manner, that it contains all that is needful for Christian knowledge and life."* That is a bold statement for such a short book! I hope that as you study Titus you will be able to discover for yourself what a treasure this book is to the church.

The Goal of this Study

The goal of this study is twofold. First, we want to spend some time noticing how the Apostle Paul describes himself and his ministry so that we might better understand the true nature of a Christ-centered ministry. This will be the essence of the first three chapters and will require us to spend a little extra time looking up verses outside of Titus so that we get a clear picture of what Paul is saying in Titus 1:1-4. Paul's brief description of himself and his work unveils certain foundational truths that we must put into practice in our own lives and ministries.

Secondly, we want to highlight the Apostle Paul's instruction as he directs Titus to strengthen the struggling church on the island of Crete. While Titus is not an exhaustive book, it is an extremely important one. The book of Titus tells us where to start in building up the Body of Christ, and how to apply the truths of the gospel message to the work of the ministry.

Bible Translation

While there are many good Bible translations, the one that we have chosen for this study is the English Standard Version. Other translations may be used with this Bible study, but there will be occasional differences where the translators chose to use a different wording to express the original Greek word. For this reason, we recommend the ESV for this study.

Preparation for Study

In a workbook format like this, there is a danger that faces the student of God's Word. You may find yourself simply skimming the verses and quickly jotting down the answers without taking any time for meditation or reflection. The goal of this study is to drive you to interact with the Scriptures and come face to face with the power of the gospel in the life of the church. If you only see the Scriptures as a "class assignment," the time spent here will be of very little benefit. If however, you remember that the Scripture is the Word of the living God, and that it must be both understood and obeyed, you will do well. May we all have the attitude of the Psalmist in the following verses:

> *Blessed is the man who walks not in the counsel of the wicked, nor stands in the way of sinners, nor sits in the seat of scoffers;* **but his delight is in the law of the LORD, and**

on his law he meditates day and night. *He is like a tree planted by streams of water that yields its fruit in its season, and its leaf does not wither. In all that he does, he prospers. (Psalm 1:1-3)*

It is through meditation and careful thought that the Word of God is allowed to nourish our souls and bear fruit in our lives. May God cause us all to be this "blessed" man described in these verses.

Chapter 1

The Church's Mission: The Great Commission

> And Jesus came and said to them, "All authority in heaven and on earth has been given to me. Go therefore and make disciples of all nations, baptizing them in the name of the Father and of the Son and of the Holy Spirit, teaching them to observe all that I have commanded you. And behold, I am with you always, to the end of the age." Matthew 28:18-20

These words from Matthew perfectly prepare the way for what we will be studying in the book of Titus. In these verses, we find some of the final instructions that our Lord gave to his disciples before he ascended to the Father. The church has historically regarded this command as the "Great Commission." These instructions answer the question that must have weighed heavy on the apostles at this time: "what next?" Jesus' words outline in incredibly simple terms what the church is to do until Christ returns:

1. Make disciples.
2. Baptize them in the name of the Father and of the Son and of the Holy Spirit.
3. Teach them to obey all that Jesus taught.

In other words, Jesus intended for his followers to "be fruitful and multiply." The gospel message that they had come to understand was for all nations! Throughout the book of Acts, we find this plan beginning to take shape as the early church was established. Not only does the gospel begin to take root in Jerusalem, but it also begins its journey to the uttermost parts of the earth. As the gospel travels through men like the apostle Paul, we notice that churches begin to gather along the way. This was not an optional, take it or leave it issue. The church is simply the natural outflow of the Great Commission itself. Notice that the Great Commission does not simply tell us to go and get huge numbers of decisions for Christ. The goal is nothing short of genuine disciples who are willing to publicly identify with Christ in baptism and then learn to obey his commands. In the local church God provides all that is necessary for this to take place.[1] It has always been God's intention for his people to gather in local churches in order to shine as lights in this dark and sinful world.

❖ *In Acts 2:38-47 we find this pattern perfectly laid out for us as Peter preaches on the day of Pentecost. What does Peter command them to do in verses 38 and 40?*

---

[1] 1 Corinthians 12:18-20 & 27 "But as it is, God arranged the members in the body, each one of them, as he chose. If all were a single member, where would the body be? As it is, there are many parts, yet one body....Now you are the body of Christ and individually members of it." In these verses, the Lord reveals the vital nature of our connection to all believers – we are a body. In a body, every part plays an important role in the overall health of the rest of the body. It is clearly absurd to think of a single member of a body trying to survive on its own and in the same way God does not intend for one believer to live independent of other believers.

❖ *What do the believers immediately begin to do after receiving his word and being baptized according to verses 42-47?*

One of these early churches was located on the island of Crete. This church was the single ray of light on an island known for its ungodliness and corruption.

In this setting Paul picks up is pen to instruct his young co-worker and son in the faith, Titus. Titus was laboring to establish this young, struggling church and Paul knew the task would not be easy. These instructions are designed to strengthen and encourage Titus as he continues the work of the Great Commission on the island of Crete.

In this letter to Titus, we find Paul simply instructing him to follow the Great Commission. Everything he tells Titus to do is designed to accomplish this end: make disciples through the preaching of the gospel and teach them to obey by giving them sound teaching. A man must believe the gospel to be a disciple, and a disciple must know what his master wants in order to obey him.

With this in mind, we now turn our attention to the opening verse of the book of Titus.

A Portrait of a Faithful Minister

Paul, a servant of God and an apostle of Jesus Christ, for the sake of the faith of God's elect and their knowledge of the truth, which accords with godliness... Titus 1:1

❖ *What two descriptions does Paul use to describe himself in this verse?*

These two words are very significant and we must understand them both clearly, if we are going to understand the nature of Paul's ministry and how it relates to us.

The first word is "servant" in our translation, and *doulos* in the original Greek. A *doulos* was a slave who was under the authority of a master. This word does not refer to someone who is paid and may come and go as he pleases, but a person who is owned by another. His life revolves completely around his master's will.

❖ *What does this tell us about the role of a gospel minister?*

❖ *If Paul is the slave, who is the master?*

Next, we find the term "apostle of Jesus Christ." The word "apostle" comes from the Greek word *apostolos* and it refers to a person who is sent out as a messenger.

❖ *Read Acts 26:12-20. What is Jesus' purpose in appearing to Paul in this way according to verse 16?*

❖ *What is Paul's mission as an apostle according to verse 18?*

Here we find Christ appointing Paul to be a witness of the resurrection, just as he had appointed the twelve. This is a very important issue, because the main qualification to be an apostle was having seen and known the resurrected Lord.[2] Through this miraculous meeting with Christ, Paul became a firsthand witness of the resurrected Lord. This was a unique calling in the early church and came with the ability to do signs and wonders.[3] These signs gave witness to the power of God and the truthfulness of the message. While we are all called to share the gospel, we rest our testimony on the Word of God that came through these men.

For the Sake of the Elect

As we read Titus 1:1, we immediately encounter the truth that Paul is laboring for the faith of God's elect. This might sound like a

---

[2] Acts 1:21-22 "So one of the men who have accompanied us during all the time that the Lord Jesus went in and out among us, beginning from the baptism of John until the day when he was taken up from us--one of these men must become with us a witness to his resurrection."

[3] Hebrews 2:3-4 "It was declared at first by the Lord, and it was attested to us by those who heard, while God also bore witness by signs and wonders and various miracles and by gifts of the Holy Spirit distributed according to his will."

peculiar statement at first, but it is packed with practical instruction for us.

The word "elect" means to be chosen or to be picked out.[4] So what does Paul mean when he says that he is an apostle for the faith of God's elect people? Does he mean that he only serves those who are already saved? Even the slightest knowledge of Paul's life and ministry reveals that this was not the case. He was constantly seeking new and unreached areas to share the gospel of Jesus Christ (Romans 15:20).[5] In 2 Timothy, we find a parallel passage that is a little more explanatory.

❖ *Read 2 Timothy 2:10. How does Paul define the goal of his ministry to the "elect" in this verse?*

In the following verses, we find a scenario where this truth becomes very practical.

❖ *Read Acts 18:9-10. In this passage, we find Paul preaching the gospel in the city of Corinth. What does God tell him in order to encourage him to keep preaching the gospel?*

---

[4] W.E. Vine, M. F. (1996). *Vine's Complete Expository Dictionary of Old and New Testament Words.* Nashville, Tennessee: Thomas Nelson.

[5] Romans 15:20 and thus I make it my ambition to preach the gospel, not where Christ has already been named, lest I build on someone's foundation,

In this account, we find Paul entering a new city to preach the gospel. The gospel was new to this area and these people were hearing the gospel for the first time. As Paul preached, he may have been tempted with discouragement by all of the persecution that he had been facing in the other cities. Yet God knew that many of those he had chosen for salvation lived in this city and they would respond to the gospel message. In these verses, the Lord uses this truth to encourage Paul to keep preaching. It is a simple fact that not everyone who will be a part of the church has heard the message yet. Someone must tell them! That is what Paul means when he says that he is an apostle for the faith of God's elect. He wanted to preach this gospel and see them turn from idols to serve the living and true God.[6]

This brings up a very important point that Paul understood clearly. Men do not build the church; God does. This is why Paul describes himself as a servant of God and an apostle of Jesus Christ. His job was not to build the church; it was much simpler than that. He was simply to obey his Master and take the message that he had been given to the world.

Read the following verses to determine how the church is built.

❖ *Acts 2:47 – What was God doing "day by day?"*

---

[6] 1Thessalonians 1:9 "For they themselves report concerning us the kind of reception we had among you, and how you turned to God from idols to serve the living and true God."

❖ *Matthew 16:18 – Who builds the church?*

It seems clear from these verses that God is the one who builds the church. He gets all the credit for the work because he builds it for his own glory. Does this mean that God will do this work without using a preacher or the gospel message? What do the following verses teach us about our role in the gospel message?

❖ *Romans 10:13-17 - What must happen before anyone will call upon the name of the Lord and how does a person gain faith?*

In these verses, we see that God does not save people without the preaching of the gospel. The fact that Christ has promised to build his church should not discourage us from being a part of evangelism. In fact, this is the best motivation to keep preaching the gospel. God has assured us that he *will* build his church. This means that people *will* respond to the gospel. Our job is simply to follow the example of Paul and preach! While we do not all share the same gift of apostleship that our brother Paul had, we must share his love for God and the church.

We must also share Paul's desire to see the church grow through the preaching of the gospel. Do we love Christ? Do we love his church? Will we preach his gospel? So many churches have lost this love for Christ and his church, and it shows in the fact that they do not speak to the lost about the Savior. This is a sure sign that God's people are drifting from their calling. A love for Christ and a love for the church will drive us to the uttermost parts of the world to preach the good news of Jesus Christ!

❖ *Read Revelation 5:9-10. How much of the world is represented in this passage?*

❖ *According to those verses, how do you think God feels about foreign missions?*

How do you feel about your Master's mission to reach the world with the gospel? Are you laboring with your gifts and abilities to see God's elect come to faith in their Savior? Or have you possibly lost contact with your Savior's heart? C.H. Spurgeon once said:

Do you want arguments for soul winning? Look up to Heaven, and ask yourself how sinners can ever reach those harps of gold and learn that everlasting song, unless they have someone to tell them of Jesus, who is mighty to save. But the best argument of all is to be found in the wounds of Jesus. You want to honor Him, you desire to put many crowns upon His head, and this you can best do by winning souls, for Him. These are the spoils that he covets, these are the trophies for which He fights, these are the jewels that shall be His best adornment.

What do the following verses teach us about God's heart for the lost?

❖ *Luke 15:1-10*

We must pause here and notice what verse 10 is actually saying. The text says that there is joy "before" the angels of God or "in the presence of" the angels of God when a sinner repents. To get the full meaning of this we must pay attention to *who* is rejoicing. The word "before" or "in the presence of" is the Greek word *enōpion*, and it refers to something which you stand face to face with or in front of.[7] It can mean "the one toward whom you turn your eyes." Therefore, it is not saying that the angels rejoice, rather it is God who rejoices![8] God's joy is on display before the angels every time a sinner repents of his sin!

❖ *Matthew 23:37 - How does Christ feel when men remain hardened in sin and rebellion?*

---

[7] W.E. Vine, M. F. (1996). *Vine's Complete Expository Dictionary of Old and New Testament Words.* Nashville, Tennessee: Thomas Nelson. (p.484)

[8] Robertson, A. T. (1930). *Word Pictures in the New Testament.* Grand Rapids, Michigan: Baker House Books. (p.207)

❖ *1 Timothy 2:1-4 - Why is it that we should pray for all men?*

What a beautiful description of God's heart! Our God delights in saving the lost souls of sinful men and he truly grieves over those who remain in sin and rebellion. This is both our example and the foundation for the Great Commission. We labor in our prayers and preaching because God is a saving God.

According to the following verses, what was Jesus' stated purpose in coming?

❖ *Luke 19:10*

❖ *Mark 1:38*

In these verses, we observe Jesus' simple explanation for coming to this earth. As we well know, Jesus did much more than preach to men; he also died and rose again for them. Without the cross, there would have been no good news to preach because every sinner would still face the punishment for his sins. However, since Jesus did die on the cross and rise again, there is good news that must be preached to all creation.[9]

❖ *In John 17:14-18, we find Jesus earnestly praying for his disciples as he nears the cross and the time of his return to his Father. According to verse 18, who would now continue his mission to seek and save the lost?*

❖ *Often we only think of the pastor, missionary, or evangelist doing the work of sharing the gospel. According to Ephesians 4:11-14, what are these leaders to do with their gifts? (v.12)*

❖ *What does it say is the ultimate goal of this work (13-14)?*

---

[9] Mark 16:15 "And he said to them, "Go into all the world and proclaim the gospel to the whole creation."

❖ Can evangelism be separated from the overall health of the local church?

❖ If a church does not evangelize, can it attain the maturity, unity, and knowledge that verse 13 says we are aiming for?

❖ We also find that personal evangelism was the normal practice of the early church members. What do Acts 8:3-4 and 11:19-21 tell us happened during the first great persecution of the church?

❖ What did Paul say about the Thessalonians in 1 Thessalonians 1:8?

From these verses, we see that Christ has commissioned his church to carry the message of the gospel to all nations. It was his mission to seek and save that which was lost, and now Christ does that work through his "body," the church. A church cannot be healthy if it is not representing Christ in this way among the nations. The world must hear the gospel through your church! This reflects a church that is in tune with its Lord. The nations must first be reached with the gospel before they can be taught all of Christ's commands and this is our Great Commission.

> And said to them, "Thus it is written, that the Christ should suffer and on the third day rise from the dead, and that repentance and forgiveness of sins should be proclaimed in his name to all nations, beginning from Jerusalem." Luke 24:46 -47

Chapter 2

The Church's Foundation: A Christ-Centered Gospel

> ¹*Paul, a servant of God and an apostle of Jesus Christ, for the sake of the faith of God's elect and their knowledge of the truth, which accords with godliness, ²in hope of eternal life, which God, who never lies, promised before the ages began ³and at the proper time manifested in his word... Titus 1:1-3a*

Having learned something of the nature and scope of gospel ministry, we now want to notice the substance of our message. Many teachers today claim to serve God and be sent by him, yet they teach a message of their own making. That is why we have such a variety of different teachings going around the church. Because of this, there is a great need for all who name the name of Christ to know and guard the truth of God's Word. In this section, we want to notice what Paul says about his message, and search the Scriptures to make sure that we are preaching the same truth that Paul preached.

❖ *What do the believers need to **know** according to Titus 1:1?*

❖ *Paul describes the nature of this truth for us. What kind of truth is it?*

Paul is clear about the message that he is preaching. He does not simply say that it is *a* "truth" or that it is *a* "gospel." Every false teacher claims he has "the truth." Paul separates his message from others by saying it is the truth which *"accords with godliness."* Godliness is the stamp that God has placed upon his truth. For every truth that God has revealed, mankind has proven that he can find a substitute that suits his lusts and allows his favorite sin. This is not the case with the true gospel. Christ told us that you shall know them by their fruits. The gospel does not condone sin with the promise of forgiveness. It draws the sinner from sin by the power of the Holy Spirit. This is what Paul means by "truth which accords with godliness." It is the truth that produces good fruit in the life of those who believe it. We learn more about this when we get to Titus 2:11-14.

According to verse 2, the knowledge of the truth is directly connected to a firmly grounded hope.

❖ *What are we hoping for?*

It would be easy for us to pass over this too quickly, but it is very important for us to catch the implications of what Paul is saying. The object of our hope will give direction to our lives. If our hope is in the wrong thing, we will go the wrong direction. We will chase after something that we are not supposed to chase after. On the other hand, if our hope is in what God has promised, then we will find ourselves chasing what is truly good and honorable. Moreover, we will actually gain what we are hoping for! A person who is chasing a lie will never have the joy of receiving what God has promised to those who believe.

❖ *Where is our hope manifested according to Titus 1:3?*

Here we find that our hope his been manifested in his "word." In other words, believers find their source of hope in the word of God. Our eternal life rests upon the unchanging word of God and is made known through faithful preaching.
Consider these verses from 1 John 1:1-3:

That which was from the beginning, which we have heard, which we have seen with our eyes, which we looked upon and have touched with our hands, concerning the word of life--the life was made manifest, and we have seen it, and testify to it and proclaim to you the eternal life, which was with the Father and was made manifest to us.

Did you notice that John said he saw and touched the "word of life"? Not only that, but he also said that he proclaimed the eternal life that was with the Father and was made manifest to him. This is obviously talking about Jesus Christ, the Son of God. He is the eternal life in which we hope. When we preach the good news of the gospel, we are telling people about *him* and what *he* has done. When people believe the gospel, they believe in him. In fact, when we say that someone has eternal life, we are also saying that the person knows God and his Son Jesus Christ (John 17:3).[10] It is impossible to preach the true gospel in a way that does not show forth the person of Christ.

> Gospel is and should be nothing else than a discourse or story about Christ. Martin Luther

Again, the "word" is the message of Christ that God has commanded us to preach. This is such an important point that we are going to spend some time looking at the "big picture" of Christ throughout the Scriptures.

All Bible-believing Christians know that Jesus was born of a virgin, lived a sinless life under the Law of God, suffered in our place on the cross, and rose again from the dead on the third day. These essentials (as well as many others) are commonly understood and agreed upon by all believers. The following study on Christ in the gospel is not intended to cover everything that could be said, but rather to emphasize essential facts about the *person* of Christ. It is far too common for those sharing the gospel to share certain historical facts yet neglect Christ himself. When this happens, Christianity can be reduced to simply agreeing with facts, as opposed to knowing God through Christ.

Sovereign Creator

Let us spend some time looking at Christ in the gospel. The message begins in Genesis with the creation of the world.

---

[10] John 17:3 "And this is eternal life, that they know you the only true God, and Jesus Christ whom you have sent."

❖ *Genesis 1:1 and John 1:1-3 - Who made the world?*

❖ *Genesis 1:31 - What was the condition of the world at that time?*

This verse points out the goodness of the one who made the world. It was good because he was good. God delighted in all he made because it was without the stain of sin and corruption.

❖ *What does Colossians 1:16-17 teach about the role of Christ in creation?*

We must understand a simple, yet essential, truth: Jesus owns everything in creation. It is his natural right as the Creator. As a result, we must conclude that all people belong to him as well.

❖ *Do most people treat Christ as if he is Lord of all?*

❖ *Does this mean that he is not Lord until someone makes him Lord or is he Lord no matter what?*

Clearly, the Scriptures teach that Jesus is the Creator God, who is equal in every way to the Father and Holy Spirit. As the Creator, he is Lord of all. No person can give him that right or take it away. It is a simple fact.

Holy Judge

Not only does the gospel exalt Christ as the Creator, it also exalts him as the Judge. We have broken his holy standard. The standard God has given us is his law. Every time we sin, we violate this law and bring condemnation on ourselves.

❖ *How does 1 John 3:4 describe sin?*

❖ *Romans 2:14-15 tells us about those who have not heard God's Word. How do they know what is right and wrong?*

❖ *Notice what Romans 2:16 says about the gospel that Paul preached. What is Christ's role?*

❖ *Many believe that God will only judge men for serious crimes like murder. Based on Romans 2:16, will any secret sins escape Christ's judgment?*

❖ *How does Revelation 19:11-16 describe Christ when he returns?*

This may be a new thought for some. Many have only seen Christ as the babe in the manger or a soft-spoken pacifist who only condemns judgment of other people. It should now be apparent that this idea could not be farther from the truth. Those who hold this idea of Christ have only half of the truth. Much of what they believe about Christ has some truth to it, yet they stop short of the full picture, either through ignorance, or because of the implications for them in their sin. They take the patience of God to mean that he will never judge. They assume that he does not mind their sin *that* much.

❖ *Read Psalm 50:16-23. What is the mistake of the wicked man in verse 21?*

According to this verse, it is exceedingly important that we have a correct view of God. On the Day of Judgment, none of us wants to be that wicked man who has brought God down to the level of his own sinfulness. This is the essence of idolatry.

In the next passage, we find Paul preaching in a city that was full of idolatry.

❖ *Notice how the nature of God is central to Paul's preaching in Acts 17:23-31. List some of the truths about God that are found in this passage.*

❖ *In verse 30, Paul makes it clear that God demands a change of direction called repentance. What is his reasoning in verse 31? Why should they repent?*

These verses teach that the truth of the coming judgment plays a major part in the gospel message.

❖ *The coming judgment is clearly described in Revelation 20:11-15. According to these verses what is the final destination for those whose names are not found in the "book of life"?*

We may look at this as "bad news" and wonder why this would be part of a message called the "good news." If this is the case, we just need to take a step back and see the big picture. It is "good news" because on the day when Christ comes back to judge, he will set everything straight. There will be a new heaven and a new earth where righteousness dwells. In the new heaven and the new earth, there will be no more suffering and no more death.[11] This is because God will remove all sin from creation, making it pure. This promise *is* good news – for the righteous. And herein lies our problem: we are not righteous.

How does the Bible describe the human race in these verses?

❖   *Isaiah 53:6*

❖   *Romans 3:10-18*

---

[11] Revelation 21:1-4 "Then I saw a new heaven and a new earth, for the first heaven and the first earth had passed away, and the sea was no more. And I saw the holy city, new Jerusalem, coming down out of heaven from God, prepared as a bride adorned for her husband. And I heard a loud voice from the throne saying, "Behold, the dwelling place of God is with man. He will dwell with them, and they will be his people, and God himself will be with them as their God. He will wipe away every tear from their eyes, and death shall be no more, neither shall there be mourning, nor crying, nor pain anymore, for the former things have passed away."

The Great Dilemma

So far, the truths that we have looked at portray a great and worthy God, but they also portray a great dilemma for us. If God is truly the Lord of all and holy and just in all of his judgments, then we can be certain that he will punish our sin. Anything else would be wicked, and this is bad news for us!

❖ *Read what Proverbs 17:15 says about justifying the guilty. How does God feel about it?*

A Glorious Savior

This is where the glory of God's *mercy* to men begins to shine. The Bible tells us that God is rich in mercy and that he has genuine love for sinners. How could love for sinners and love for righteousness meet? Many people believe that God's love cancels his righteousness, but this is not true at all. God did not choose his love over his goodness, rather he upheld them both perfectly in his plan to save sinners. This is the glory of the cross! The cross of Jesus Christ is where both love and righteousness met in perfect harmony and God brought salvation to men.

❖ *Read Isaiah 53:4-6. What was Christ's work of love on the cross?*

❖ *Were we seeking his favor or acting like his enemies?*

❖ *What does 1 Corinthians 15:1-4 tell us about the gospel? Specifically, what were the three parts of Christ's work? (vv. 3-4)*

❖ *How does 2 Corinthians 5:21 explain what happened on the cross? What did Christ become on our behalf?*

❖ *What do we become in him?*

This verse is such a beautiful description of what Christ did to redeem us from our sin! When it says he became sin for us, it simply means that he was treated as if he had committed *our* sins. The innocent One was punished in the place of the guilty.

Not only that, but we also see that we who believe become the righteousness of God *in him*. This does not mean that we become perfectly righteous in ourselves, but rather that we are *treated as if* we had done all of his good works. Our hope of eternal life is not that we have been good enough, but rather that Christ was good enough in our place. When we believe in him, we are covered with his good works, not our own.

❖ *Read Romans 3:23-30. What does verse 23 say about us?*

❖ *How does verse 24 say we can be justified (declared righteous)?*

❖ *How does verse 28 tell us that this gift of justification is received?*

This is why Spurgeon exclaimed:

Oh! It is my soul's delight to preach a gospel which has an open door to it, to preach a mercy-seat which has no veil before it; the veil is rent in twain, and now the biggest sinner out of hell who desires to come, is welcome.[12]

---

[12] Spurgeon, C.(2012,AprilWednesday) .*Metropolitan Tabernacle Pulpit.* Retrieved from Spurgeon Archive: http://www.spurgeon.org/sermons/0581.htm

Coming King

Not only is Christ the sovereign Creator, holy Judge, and glorious Savior, he is also our coming King! The promise of the gospel is that Christ is returning for his church, which he refers to as his Bride. Notice the promises that we have been given:

❖ *What was the angel's promise to the disciples when Jesus ascended to the Father in Acts 1:10-11?*

❖ *According to Philippians 3:20-21, where is our home and what is our hope?*

❖ *According to Hebrews 9:28, what is Christ coming for the second time?*

❖ *What instructions do we find in 1 Peter 1:13 as we wait for this glorious hope?*

❖ *Read 1 Thessalonians 1:9-10. Describe the change in the life of these believers.*

❖ *How is this hope described in verse 10?*

This brings us full circle to Titus 1:1-3. The gospel is "the truth which accords with godliness, in hope of eternal life, which God, who never lies, promised before the ages began...."

The Proper Response

This means that there is no way that our good works can possibly make us righteous in God's sight. Only the righteousness that Jesus freely gives can make us worthy of eternal life. The question that faces everyone who has heard the gospel is simple, "Will you repent of your sin and receive Jesus Christ the Lord?" It is not enough to simply believe right facts about Christ (James 2:19).[13] Saving faith goes beyond knowing who he is to actually receiving him for who he is. This is why the Bible often uses repentance as a synonym for saving faith. When we truly believe in Christ, we repent (have a change of mind) toward Christ. If there is no change of mind, there will be no change in our direction. We will continue to live lives of rebellion against our Savior and King. Many people throughout history have known who Christ was, yet

---

[13] James 2:19 "You believe that God is one; you do well. Even the demons believe--and shudder!"

they never received him as their Lord and Savior because of the dramatic change that it would bring into their lives. Others have claimed to believe, yet they live out lives of rebellion against Christ and prove that they have never truly repented of their sin and received the Savior.

> But to all who did receive him, who believed in his name, he gave the right to become children of God. (John 1:12)

Chapter 3

The Church's Power: The Preaching of the Gospel

> [1]Paul, a servant of God and an apostle of Jesus Christ, for the sake of the faith of God's elect and their knowledge of the truth, which accords with godliness, [2]in hope of eternal life, which God, who never lies, promised before the ages began [3]and at the proper time manifested in his word through the preaching with which I have been entrusted by the command of God our Savior... Titus 1:1-3

As we have just seen, the gospel Paul preached was specific; it is the gospel of Christ! Paul perfectly sums it up as the "gospel of the glory of Christ, who is the image of God" (2 Corinthians 4:4).[14] What could be clearer? The gospel is about the glory of Christ. When we preach the gospel, Christ should shine forth!

In this chapter, we move from the content of this message to the power of this message. While this may seem like a small part of our text, it is a large part of gospel ministry, and we must not miss this foundational truth.

---

[14] 2 Corinthians 4:4 " In their case the god of this world has blinded the minds of the unbelievers, to keep them from seeing the light of the gospel of the glory of Christ, who is the image of God. "

❖ *According to verse 3, what has God entrusted to Paul by sovereign command?*

The message that Paul preached was entrusted to him as a sacred charge. The Greek word for "preaching" is *kerugma,* and it refers to a proclamation by a herald. In that day, it was a common practice for a king to issue a decree to his kingdom. This was done by a herald who was charged with delivering the decree by announcing it to the people of the kingdom. The job was simple, stand up and proclaim the message of the king. This is what God commissioned Paul to do. God gave him this proclamation (or preaching) and his one task was to proclaim it.

❖ *Was this "preaching" an invention of Paul's ingenuity?*

❖ *Where did it come from?*

The proclamation of this message was not Paul's idea. It was not something popular in that day, nor was it a clever technique for persuasion. It was simply the command of God. In 1 Corinthians 9:16, Paul says, "For if I preach the gospel, that gives me no ground for boasting. For necessity is laid upon me. Woe to me if I preach not the gospel!" Paul clearly understood what it meant to be entrusted with the preaching of the Word of God. The question is, do *we* understand what it means to be entrusted with that message? Do we understand that, as the church, God has entrusted us with the truth of the gospel, and that this gospel must be proclaimed to all creation? Surely we all have different gifts to use in this cause, but let us not forget the cause! It is the discipling of all nations by the proclamation of the gospel.

To get a better understanding of the primary role of gospel preaching in the building up and strengthening of the church, we must spend some time looking at other Scriptures. These Scriptures will give us a proper appreciation for this brief statement in Titus 1:3.

> ❖ *Read 2 Timothy 4:1-2. Here we find Paul giving his final instructions to his young co-worker Timothy. What is Paul's charge to Timothy in verse 2?*

Paul labors to drive home the urgency of this charge. He does not just charge Timothy with this responsibility, but he charges him "*in the presence of God and Christ Jesus who is to judge the living and the dead, and by his appearing and his kingdom.*" One cannot imagine a more solemn charge. To disregard Paul's exhortation would be to disregard all that the Christian faith holds most sacred. Surely, this was not just *a* priority, but *the* priority of his ministry.

❖ *The charge to preach is explained in verse 2. What other actions are included in the charge to preach the Word?*

This makes it clear that preaching includes the full communication of God's truth. It includes both negative rebuke and positive exhortation. It includes readiness at a moment's notice as well as patience in teaching when we see little or no fruit. We find the reason for such a solemn charge in the unique power that God has chosen to place in the gospel message itself.

❖ *How does Romans 1:16 refer to the gospel?*

This may sound like an overstatement for effect at first. Does he really mean to say that the simple message of Jesus dead, buried, and risen, bringing us to repentance and forgiveness of sins is powerful in itself? Yes!

❖ *Read 1 Corinthians 1:17-24. What did Christ send Paul to preach in verse 17?*

❖ *According to verse 18, how did the world feel about the message?*

❖ *What was the effect on those who were being saved in verse 18?*

❖ *According to verses 19-20, what was the God-ordained purpose behind the "folly of what we preach"?*

❖ *Based on verse 21, can man know God through human wisdom?*

❖ *What means does God use to save men? (v.21)*

Notice that the knowledge of God comes, not *in spite of* the folly of what we preach, but *through* the folly of what we preach. There is something special going on in these verses. It is not that the message itself is foolish, but that the message is foolish to those who are lost. Without conviction of sin, the message does not meet the perceived needs of those in the world. It does not give them the worldly status or comfort that they are looking for. Yet, to those who know their sin separates them from eternal life with God, it is a hidden treasure that supplies all they need. This truth is very practical and it affected how Paul preached.

❖ *Notice what 1 Corinthians 2:1-5 says about how not to preach the gospel. What did Paul refuse to use in preaching?*

❖ *What was the one thing that Paul decided to know and preach? (v.2)*

❖ *Why did he do this? (v.5)*

What does Paul mean when he says he refused to use lofty speech or wisdom? Does it mean that he used bad grammar and was hard to understand on purpose? No, Paul was a smart man and he was very clear when he preached the gospel. We can read it and understand it just fine. What he is saying is that he did not adjust the gospel to be more acceptable to the "wise" Gentiles. He did not adjust the gospel for fear of offending the Jews who hated

Christ. He simply made Christ known by preaching God's word without adjustment. The offense that comes with it is part of its power. The gospel offends the wise by telling them that their wisdom is foolish to God, and it offends the self-righteous by telling them that they are sinners in God's eyes. If we lose these truths, we lose the gospel.

What do the following verses say about God's Word?

❖ *Romans 10:17 - Where does faith come from?*

In this verse, we learn that faith is brought to human hearts through the hearing of the Word of Christ. In the following verses, we see the same amazing truth described in a different way.

❖ *Read 1 Peter 1:23-25. What is the seed that has brought the new birth to believers?*

❖ *How is it described?*

❖ *What does verse 25 say about the Word of the Lord?*

❖ *According to verse 25, how did God plant his word in their hearts?*

These verses explain why preaching is central to gospel ministry. It is through the preaching of the gospel that God plants his word in people's hearts. Just as the life of each plant begins with the seed, in the same way eternal life begins with the seed of the gospel message entering the human heart. Without the preaching of the Word of God there is no seed to grow and life is impossible. On the other hand, when God's word is faithfully and accurately proclaimed, the seed of eternal life is sown into human hearts, thus bringing salvation to all who receive it.

So far, we have only looked at verses that describe the Word of God as it brings new life or salvation. Does that mean that God's Word has no function after conversion? Is it just to bring about the one time transformation, or is there a continuing work that the Word does as we grow in our faith?

What do these verses say about the work of the Word in the life of the believer?

❖ *1 Thessalonians 2:13 - Who is God's Word working in?*

❖ *1 Peter 2:1-2 - The Word of God is often compared to nourishing food (Matthew 4:4; Hebrews 5:12-14). What is the effect of this pure spiritual milk?*

❖ *Colossians 1:5-6 – What is the gospel doing in the lives of the believers?*

❖ *Read John 17:17. What is it that sanctifies (sets believers apart from the world to be like Christ)?*

These passages teach that the Word of God is the source of every good change in the life of the believer. Do we want to be mature in our faith, bear good fruit, and be more holy? The tool God uses to do this work in our lives is the same. It is the Word of God. In fact, it is important to notice that in Colossians 1:5-6, we are specifically told that the gospel is doing this work in our lives. We must understand that the truths of the gospel message are not simply beginner level truths that we move past as we grow in our faith. On the contrary, we must go deeper into these truths if we want to go higher in maturity. This means that godly men must preach it thoroughly and faithfully. This was Paul's calling, and it is still the calling of every gospel minister today. Martin Luther said, "To preach Christ is to feed the soul, to justify it, to set it free, to save it, if it believes the preaching."[15]

---

[15] Luther, Martin (2006-02-26). Concerning Christian Liberty (p. 11). Public Domain Books. Kindle Edition.

❖ *In conclusion, go back to Titus 1:3. How is God described at the end of verse 3?*

It is easy for us to see the salvation of souls as our work. Yet this passage leaves no room for that. It was God who promised the hope of eternal life long ages ago and God who manifested it at the proper time. It was Christ who chose and sent out men to be witnesses of his resurrection. Moreover, it was God who entrusted this sacred proclamation to the apostle Paul. God is a saving God. Salvation is purely his work. This is an essential truth to grasp because it will affect how we seek to do the work of the ministry. If we see the salvation of souls as primarily our job, we will scramble around seeking to find something that works and gets results. If, however, we see salvation as God's work from beginning to end, we will simply do the part God has commanded us to do, whether or not we think it is working. May this truth focus our efforts by directing our attention to the simple proclamation of gospel truth, and may it encourage us in our labors, knowing God will use his Word.

So shall my word be that goes out from my mouth; it shall not return to me empty, but it shall accomplish that which I purpose, and shall succeed in the thing for which I sent it.
Isaiah 55:11

Chapter 4

Establish Godly Leadership

> *⁴To Titus, my true child in a common faith: Grace and peace from God the Father and Christ Jesus our Savior. ⁵This is why I left you in Crete, so that you might put what remained into order, and appoint elders in every town as I directed you.*
> Titus 1:4-5

Having looked at the nature and purpose of the ministry, we now turn our attention to the instructions for building up the local church. As we have noted already in the introduction, Titus is on the island of Crete serving a young, struggling church. We do not know how or when the gospel first came to the island, but we do know that Paul and Titus had been there together for a time. The references in this book are the only information we have about this particular trip by Paul and Titus. This trip is not mentioned in any of the missionary journeys recorded in the book of Acts, so most scholars believe that this trip took place after Paul was released from his Roman captivity at the end of that book. We do not know why Paul did not stay longer, but we do learn what Titus was supposed to do while he was there.

❖ *According to verse 5, what was the first reason that Titus was left in Crete?*

The word for "put in order" is a term that implies setting something straight for healing (as in a broken bone).[16] This picture of health reoccurs throughout Titus in reference to teaching or doctrine. A healthy church cannot grow out of unhealthy doctrine.

❖ *What is Paul's second instruction for Titus?*

❖ *Where was Titus to appoint elders?*

❖ *Based on this information, do you think that it is important for churches to have elders*

---

[16] Marvin R. Vincent, D. (1904). *Vincent's Word Studies in the New Testament Part Four.* New York: Charles Scribner's Sons.(p.333)

As we will see in the coming verses, a local church must have leadership. God has always ordained leaders to guide and protect his people. From families to nations to the church, we find that leadership is an essential element in God's plan for human relationships.

❖ *What does Hebrews 13:17 say about the responsibility of the leaders in the church?*

❖ *What does this passage tell us about the church member's responsibility to the leaders?*

These commands can only be obeyed when people are committed to a specific local church and its leaders. God does not intend for believers to wander around as spiritual nomads, occasionally bumping into other believers along the way. Instead, God has ordained for his people to gather in local congregations for worship, teaching, fellowship, prayer, and encouragement. It is only in these local churches that men and women can make sense out of these commands for shepherds and their flocks. We must all take heed of the following instructions from Hebrews 10:24-25:

And let us consider how to stir up one another to love and good works, not neglecting to meet together, as is the habit of some, but encouraging one another, and all the more as you see the Day drawing near.

❖ *Look carefully at the last phrase of Titus 1:5. Were these new instructions for Titus?*

It is obvious that these instructions were nothing new for Paul's faithful co-worker in the ministry. It appears that this exhortation was given to strengthen Titus' authority as he tried to accomplish this difficult task. This letter made it clear that he was not following his own opinions, but the commands of an apostle of Jesus Christ. This letter functions in the same way for us. We do not have to rest on our opinions of what is important in church ministry, but simply make sure that we are following the instructions handed down to us in the Scriptures.

The Elder and His Character

> [6] *... [I]f anyone is above reproach, the husband of one wife, and his children are believers and not open to the charge of debauchery or insubordination. [7]For an overseer, as God's steward, must be above reproach. He must not be arrogant or quick-tempered or a drunkard or violent or greedy for gain, [8]but hospitable, a lover of good, self-controlled, upright, holy, and disciplined. Titus 1:6-8*

So what is an elder? The Greek word here is *preshuteros*, and literally means one who is older in years. Yet it is also used to refer to those of any age who are in a position of leadership.[17] It is used of the forefathers of Israel in Hebrews 11:2[18] and here of those who would act as fathers in the church. It clearly refers to those who hold a respected leadership position in the church.

❖ *What is the other word that we find used in verse 7?*

The Greek word for "overseer" is *episkopos,* and simply refers to one who "watches over" or "oversees." Since this is talking about the same position in the church as an elder, we can see that this position is one of watchful care over God's people. In 1 Peter 5:1-2, we see this oversight referred to as "shepherding."[19] The word "shepherd" gives a beautiful picture of the loving care and leadership that God requires from those who are elders.

Before a man can be entrusted with the care of God's precious flock, he must be qualified. The first thing that Paul emphasizes is the need for godly character in the life of the elder. As with every other part of life and ministry, this qualification springs directly out of the gospel. The true gospel is a transforming gospel. No person who has come to see the glory of Christ and embrace him by faith can remain the same. They are a new creation! If the goal is to lead by example, as Peter says, then the elder must be an example of this new life. His life must reflect the transforming power of God's grace. These requirements are not only for the

---

[17] W.E. Vine, M. F. (1996). *Vine's Complete Expository Dictionary of Old and New Testament Words.* Nashville, Tennessee: Thomas Nelson. (p.195)

[18] Hebrews 11:2 "For by it the elders obtained a good report."(KJV)

[19] 1Peter 5:1-3 So I exhort the elders among you, as a fellow elder and a witness of the sufferings of Christ, as well as a partaker in the glory that is going to be revealed: shepherd the flock of God that is among you,...but being examples to the flock.

elder, but should be true for every mature believer. The elder must simply live like a Christian.

The nature of these requirements also springs from the nature of the church's commission. God has called us to make disciples and teach them to observe all that Jesus commanded. How could the elder possibly do this if he does not know or obey Christ? The elder must be a man who models obedience as much as he teaches obedience.

The qualities listed in verses 6-8 can be divided into two parts: an elder must be faithful *in* his home and he must be faithful *outside* his home.

In verse 6, we see that he must be above reproach with regard to his home. In our day, this might be one of the most overlooked qualities among pastors and elders, yet this is not optional. Surely, we must extend grace to our leaders and we understand that this is not speaking of perfection. Yet sadly, we often see cases where the worst children in the church belong to the leadership.

❖ *How does Paul describe being above reproach in one's home? - Titus 1:6*

The quality of being a husband of one wife is often interpreted to mean that the man cannot be divorced. A literal reading of "a husband of one wife," is a *one-woman man*. This passage does not refer to divorce but to the man's faithfulness in marriage. Paul is explaining that marital faithfulness is a non-negotiable for an elder.

When we think of having children who are believers, it is important to note that the word "believing" can also be translated "faithful." Many prefer this reading because the Scriptures teach that we are not ultimately in control of who believes and who does not. Either way, we see that the elder is to be a proven leader in his home. This will be evident in the behavior of his children.

❖ *What does 1 Timothy 3:5 tell us about the reason for requiring these qualities in an elder?*

Today many men seem to justify neglecting their families for the ministry. They feel that they are sacrificing to please God.

❖ *According to the biblical instructions in these two passages, what does the Bible teach us about neglecting one's family for any reason?*

Every man who has a family has a ministry already. If he is not faithful to that ministry, he cannot justify that sin with great victories in a public ministry. Showmanship in public ministry is often mistaken for faithfulness. Our ministry in the hidden areas reveals our true character. May every man in the church take this seriously!

In verse 7, we find the second reference to being above reproach. This time Paul describes virtues related to overall character.

❖ *What qualities do verses 7 and 8 lay out for the elder?*

1.

2.

3.

4.

5.

6.

7.

8

9.

10.

11.

12.

Now that you have listed the negative and positive qualities, go through them and write down the opposite characteristic beside each one. As you do this, ask yourself what damage each of these sins could do to the ministry, as well as the blessing these qualities would bring to the ministry.

These are simply the normal character traits for a Christian. A godly elder will be able to do more than explain what the Christian life looks like. He will be able to *show* what the Christian life looks like.

Listen to the following word of exhortation from Richard Baxter:

Take heed to yourselves, lest your example contradict your doctrine, and lest you lay such stumbling-blocks before the blind, as may be the occasion of their ruin; lest you unsay with your lives what you say with your tongues.[20]

Sound Doctrine

> *He must hold firm to the trustworthy word as taught, so that he may be able to give instruction in sound doctrine and also to rebuke those who contradict it. Titus 1:9*

While a godly character is absolutely necessary in the life of an elder, it is not the only quality that he must possess.

❖ *What requirement does Paul add to the quality of Christ-like character in verse 9?*

This second requirement has to do with faithfulness to the Word of God. In one sense, this is also a godly character trait, but it is more than that. It is an issue of knowledge. The man must be convinced that he is charged with a sacred ministry – the ministry of the Word. He must be as unwavering as Paul was when he said that he was committed to preaching Christ in a world that thought it was evil or foolish.[21] In just the same way, every elder must stand firm on God's Word. It is easy to think that Paul was extraordinary in his commitment to God's Word because he was such a great apostle. This is not true. If the church is to remain the church, there must be men in every generation and in every church who stand just as firmly upon God's Word.

---

[20] Baxter, R. (2007). *The Reformed Pastor.* Carlisle, Pennsylvania: Banner of Truth Trust. (p.63)

[21] See discussion on pages 41 and 42.

❖ *Paul is very clear about why this is such a vital issue for those who will be leading the church. What is the two-fold reason that we find in Titus 1:9?*

It is a sad reality that there are many false teachers and false teachings that have plagued the church in every generation. This is exactly what Paul is concerned about in this passage. Throughout the centuries, many pastors have neglected this aspect of ministry only to find themselves or their congregations drifting into false doctrine and heresy. A false gospel can be accepted and believed with unbelievable ease and comfort. In the following passage, we see the apostle Paul's godly example and warning to a group of elders.

❖ *Read Acts 20:26-31. How did Paul show his faithfulness to these elders and the Word of God in verse 27?*

❖ *What command does he give them in verse 28?*

❖ *What is the danger that he warns of in verse 29?*

❖ *What is the danger that he warns of in verse 30?*

The seriousness of this reality drives home the need for every church leader to guard the sacred charge of the gospel. If they do not hold fast to the "trustworthy word as taught," the false teacher could be them!

❖ *This is the same truth that we see in 1 Timothy 4:13-16. What is Timothy to give special attention to in verse 13?*

❖ *What are the two main issues that Paul commands Timothy to "keep watch on" in his own life? (v.16)*

In all of these passages, we see the common thread of personal godliness and faithful proclamation of God's Word. Again, we see the power of the Word working *in* the man to make him holy, and *through* the man to make the church holy. What a great charge!

Having seen the greatness of the task, let us always remember that our sufficiency must come from Christ!

❖ *What does Paul say about our sufficiency in 2 Corinthians 3:5-6?*

This should encourage the humble minister and humble the proud minister. It should encourage the humble because he does not have to be great or powerful. He simply has to tell people what God has said, and by God's grace, be an example of a Christian.

On the other hand, it should humble the proud minister by taking all the credit from him. The ministry is not built on the greatness of the man but on the greatness of the gospel. If he is seeking self-exaltation, he will find only condemnation.

> *Keep a close watch on yourself and on the teaching. Persist in this, for by so doing you will save both yourself and your hearers. 1 Timothy 4:16*

Chapter 5

Boldly Oppose False Teaching

> ^{9}He must hold firm to the trustworthy word as taught, so that he may be able to give instruction in sound doctrine and also rebuke those who contradict it. ^{10}For there are many who are insubordinate, empty talkers and deceivers, especially those of the circumcision party. ^{11}They must be silenced, since they are upsetting whole families by teaching for shameful gain what they ought not to teach. ^{12} One of the Cretans, a prophet of their own, said, "Cretans are always liars, evil beasts, lazy gluttons. ^{13}This testimony is true. Therefore rebuke them sharply, that they may be sound in the faith, ^{14}not devoting themselves to Jewish myths and the commands of people who turn away from the truth. Titus 1:9-14

As we read these instructions from the apostle Paul, we cannot help but notice a sense of danger as he talks about false teaching. The reason for this is simple - the health of a church flows directly from its healthy doctrine. Spiritual life and maturity do not come from how earnestly we believe something to be true, but from the truth of what we believe. This is why the church must guard this treasure of sound teaching with such great care. Paul makes it clear that a healthy church does not come about by accident, and it does not stay healthy without hard work. In every healthy church, there must be a courageous fight against false doctrine on every side. In the last chapter, we learned of the need for godly leaders who will bravely accept this responsibility.

This brings us to the difficult task now facing Titus and the elders that he would appoint. First, we will notice what these verses tell us about the challenges facing these churches, and then we will turn our attention to the instructions that Paul gives.

❖ *In Titus 1:10 we find Paul describing the false teachers who were making their way into the church. How does Paul describe these men in verse 10?*

In Titus 1:10 and the verses that follow, the main emphasis is on the character of the false teachers, not their doctrine. In fact, it appears that there was more than one source of false doctrine since Paul says, "especially those of the circumcision party." This implies that there were other false teachings floating around as well. However, this teaching by the circumcision party seems to be the main issue, since verse 14 continues to describe their false teaching.

So what is the circumcision party? Here Paul is referring to the sect that taught salvation came only through strict adherence to the Mosaic Law *and* faith in Christ. There was a heavy emphasis on circumcision, which was the sign of God's covenant with Abraham and the Jewish people. By submitting to this ritual, they were placing themselves under the Mosaic covenant, with all of its laws and requirements. By doing this, they were choosing to hold on to the Old Covenant (or agreement) that God had made with the Jewish people, and they were rejecting the New Covenant that Jesus had brought. They wanted to hold on to the temporary sacrifices and rituals of the Old Covenant and mix that with the work of Jesus on the cross. In Galatians 5:1-6, Paul calls this a rejection of the perfect work of Christ and the New Covenant that he had purchased with his blood. [22] It was the same as saying that Christ's death was not enough to pay for our sin. By failing to trust in the perfect work of Christ, these people fell under the condemnation of the Old Covenant law.

❖ *According to Galatians 3:10, what does God say about those who rely on the works of the law?*

❖ *What was the purpose of the law (Old Covenant) according to Galatians 3:24?*

Obviously, this false teaching had spread to the island of Crete and was corrupting this young church as it was just beginning to grow.

❖ *In Titus 1:11, Paul reveals what was motivating these false teachers. Why do they teach what they do?*

---

[22] Galatians 5:2&4 Look: I, Paul, say to you that if you accept circumcision, Christ will be of no advantage to you. You are severed from Christ, you who would be justified by the law; you have fallen away from grace.

Sadly, this is a common theme in the New Testament and throughout church history. Men who enter the ministry and prosper as false teachers always have an ulterior motive. Since they do not know God and do not care about God's glory, their motivation comes from greed and self-gratification. There are too many verses on this topic in the New Testament to look at them all, but it is important enough that we will take a short look at some of them here.

Look up the following verses and make note of the way the false teachers are described in these verses.

❖ *Philippians 3:18-19*

❖   *2 Peter 2:1-3*

In these verses, we see the picture of men who live for and serve the lusts of their flesh. There is no fear of God in their hardened hearts. In fact, they are men who actually deny their Master, who is Christ Jesus. Listen to these sobering words to pastors from Richard Baxter:

Believe it, sirs, God is no respecter of persons: he saveth not men for their coats or callings; a holy calling will not save an unholy man.[23]

As we have seen in the life and example of the apostle Paul, all true ministers are slaves of one Master. The true believer and the true minister serve Christ, although very imperfectly. On the other hand, the false convert and false teacher serve only their lusts and pleasures. This is what drives them and it will be what destroys them in the end.

In Titus 1:12, we find a quote from one of the pagan prophets named Epimenides. He lived during the 6th – 5th century B.C., and the description that he gave of the island of Crete was less than flattering.

❖ *How does this pagan prophet describe the culture?*

❖ *Was this just a problem out in the world or had this problem come to affect the church as well?*

It appears that the unrestrained lifestyle of the culture was seriously affecting the church. In these verses, we begin to see a connection between false teaching and unrighteous living. Paul has already made it clear that faithful doctrine is the foundation of godly living; here he makes a direct connection between false

---

[23] Baxter, R. (2007). *The Reformed Pastor.* Carlisle, Pennsylvania: Banner of Truth Trust. (p.73)

teaching and ungodly living as well. It works both ways. Consider the wise counsel of C. H Spurgeon:

> "Hold fast the form of sound words," *because error in doctrine almost inevitably leads to error in practice.* When a man believes wrongly, he will soon act wrongly. Faith has a great influence on our conduct. As a man's faith, so is he. If you begin to imbibe erroneous doctrines, they will soon have an effect on your practice.[24]

It is important to notice that the false teachers were leading them back to the law to find salvation. Yet instead of becoming holy, they were becoming more wicked and worldly. This will always be the case when men try to use the works of the law to achieve holiness. The law has no power to save us; it simply demands obedience and punishment for all who fall short.

❖ *What damaging effects of false doctrine do we find in Titus 1:11?*

It is interesting to note that entire families were being led astray by this false teaching. We know that one requirement for being an elder was to have believing children. Could it be that this is an indictment of the fathers who did not protect their households? Paul clearly taught that a man had to prove he could protect his own house from false teaching if he was going to be trusted as an elder in the household of God.

---

[24] Spurgeon, C. (2007). *The New Park Street Pulpit Vol.1&2*. Grand Rapids, Michigan: Baker Books. (p.204)

❖ *In Titus 1:9-13, Paul gives instructions for dealing with false teaching. What are the responses to false teaching that we see in verses 9, 11, and 13?*

❖ *Who was responsible to carry out these commands?*

These verses give us the biblical method for dealing with false teachers and their teaching. There is no dialogue with these men or debating over the truth. They were to be openly rebuked and stopped. The word for "silenced" in verse 11 means to muzzle. This is a very vivid description of how to deal with false teachers. In this situation, we also see that there is a need for "sharp rebuke" according to verse 13.

❖ *In verse 13, we see Paul telling Titus to rebuke them sharply. What is the purpose?*

The goal is never to harm God's flock, but rather to bring them healing and safety. The reason for such harsh rebuke in this situation springs from the severe nature of the problem. False teaching always brings about destruction and wickedness, while leaving men in darkness and without hope. Not only that, but it spreads like a disease throughout the church.

❖ *What does Paul say about those who teach these false "gospels" in Galatians 1:6-9?*

It should be apparent that every elder has a grave responsibility to oppose false teaching for the health and strength of the church. The following are passages of Scripture that address this issue.

❖ *Unfortunately, there will be times when an elder in the church is found in sin or false teaching. How does 1 Timothy 5:19-20 tell us to deal with elders who are in sin?*

❖ *Read Galatians 2:14 and notice what takes place between the apostle Peter (Cephas) and the apostle Paul. Based on what we see here, is anyone in the church too important to rebuke publicly?*

❖ *Peter was not in any obvious moral sin, yet his actions were hindering the gospel. What did Paul accuse him of? (v.14 a)*

This kind of correction only applies to those who are teaching severe error and leading others astray. The necessity becomes obvious when we understand the immense dangers involved in false teaching.

❖ *In all this talk about rebuking and correcting, one might imagine an abrasive and harsh tone. What does 2 Timothy 2:24-25 tell us about the proper way to approach the false teachers?*

❖ *According to these verses, what are we hoping for when we correct someone who is opposing the truth?*

This passage clarifies how an elder must deal with those who oppose the truth, but this does not mean false teaching should be dealt with lightly in the church. It is possible to say and do hard things in a spirit of gentleness and humility, and that is our calling.

The Root of the Problem

> [15]To the pure, all things are pure, but to the defiled and unbelieving, nothing is pure; but both their minds and their consciences are defiled. [16]They profess to know God, but they deny him by their works. They are detestable, disobedient, unfit for any good work. Titus 1:15-16

In these verses, Paul strikes at the heart of their false doctrine. They were seeking to be pure through outward rituals of the Old Covenant. They thought that ceremonies and sacrifices would take away sin and make them pure, but they had completely misunderstood what true cleansing was. They seemed to believe that true cleansing was a matter of refraining from certain outward activities, along with the outward washings and cleansings of animal sacrifices. They saw certain outward things as unclean and defiling. This drove them to refrain from touching or tasting certain foods, or even certain people. They did not realize that the laws and outward ceremonies were all telling the story of the gospel. Every moral command that God gave them revealed their inability to be holy as God is holy. Furthermore, every sacrifice and ceremony revealed a living picture of God's glorious salvation through Jesus Christ. The Old Covenant paved the way for and preached the gospel.

❖ *According to verse 15, what is it that makes all things pure?*

The "pure" is referring to those who have been washed by the sacrifice of God's Lamb, Jesus Christ. They no longer have to seek some other means of cleansing. They no longer have to observe the pictures of the gospel (the Old Covenant). They are perfectly pure through their **faith** in Christ. They are free! Not free to sin but free from the bondage of the law's condemnation. We are also free from obligation to the rituals and ceremonies that pointed to Christ. Today the church no longer celebrates these rituals and ceremonies in light of the finished work of Christ. In their place we observe baptism and the Lord's supper as we celebrate the blessings of the New Covenant that Christ purchased with his blood. Yet even in these celebrations, we must understand that they do not save us any more than the ceremonies of the Old Covenant saved the Israelites. They are all pictures of what Christ has done for us not what we have done for him.

❖ *How are those who are **not pure** described in verse 15?*

❖ *What do the impure profess with their mouths?*

❖ *What do the they say with their works?*

While these men may make great boasts of their knowledge of God and disciplined observance of the Law, they prove themselves to be liars in the end. They may not only point to the ceremonies but other good works like fasting, prayer and giving to the poor. While these are all good things to do, we must let Paul's plain statements sink in.

❖ *How does Paul describe those who profess to know God but deny him by their deeds?*

The message is clear. A man can say as many words or do as many "good deeds" as he wants, but he cannot earn God's favor. "Augustine well said, 'Good works, as they are called, in sinners, are nothing but splendid sins.'"[25]

The false teachers (and many today) misunderstand one crucial issue. They do not understand where the root of sin originates. They see sin and defilement as something that comes from the outside.

❖ *Where does Jesus say that sin and defilement come from in Mark 7:20-23?*

When Jesus says that these things come from the heart of man, he is referring to the doctrine of "original sin." While this is not popular today, it is very difficult to deny. Men are born with a nature that is sinful and enjoys its own sinfulness. It is extremely important for us to understand where our defilement comes from.

It should be apparent that these false teachers are not a special class of sinner. The only thing that sets the godly elder or church member apart from the ungodly is the renewing work of God in

---

[25] Charles Haddon Spurgeon (2009-08-19). Spurgeon's Sermons Volume 2: 1856 - Enhanced Version (Kindle Locations 3888-3889). Christian Classics Ethereal Library. Kindle Edition.

his or her life. The only pure people in the world are those who have been redeemed by Christ and "born again" by the power of the Holy Spirit. We will see this work discussed in chapter 3 of Titus.

❖ *Where does the change have to take place – on the inside or on the outside?*

This is an incredibly important point in our theology. We must understand the correct relationship between faith and works. Works are not the main issue. The reason a man is lost is always, without exception, that he has a sinful heart and is inwardly defiled. The heart of man is what must change. Works will either confirm or deny the claim that we have been born again, but they cannot make us born again. Only the Holy Spirit can make a man a new creation with new desires.

Remember, these false teachers were very religious! The problem was that they were also unbelieving. Apart from faith in Christ, a man cannot please God. As we have seen, man's greatest problem is within himself. It appears that these false teachers were turning back to the works of the Law to make themselves right with God. Yet in doing that, they made it evident that they had no real faith in Christ. Their faith was in their own ability to be good and please God by the law. They thought rituals and ceremonies could bring purity, but only the work of Christ can bring the purity that God requires. The man who wants to be pure must trust the Savior and no other.

It is these who cause divisions, worldly people, devoid of the Spirit. But you, beloved, building yourselves up in your most holy faith and praying in the Holy Spirit, keep yourselves in the love of God, waiting for the mercy of our Lord Jesus Christ that leads to eternal life. Jude 1:19-21

Chapter 6

Teach Gospel-Centered Living in the Church

> But as for you, teach what accords with sound doctrine.... that the word of God may not be reviled....so that an opponent may be put to shame, having nothing evil to say about us....so that in everything they may adorn the doctrine of God our Savior. Titus 2:1,5,8 & 10

Paul now turns his attention from the leadership to the members of the congregation. Throughout Titus chapter two, we find the instructions for gospel-centered living within the church. Paul specifically addresses each member of the household as he challenges them to live in a way that is fitting for sound doctrine.

So what exactly is the sound doctrine that Paul is talking about? This term simply refers to the gospel in its broadest scope. Matthew Henry describes it in the following way when commenting on this passage:

> The true doctrines of the gospel are *sound doctrines*...they are in themselves good and holy, and make the believers so; they make them fit for, and vigorous in, the service of God.[26]

---

[26] Henry, Matthew (2010-11-07). Unabridged Matthew Henry's Commentary on the Whole Bible (best navigation) (Kindle Locations 290351-290353). OSNOVA. Kindle Edition.

In our passage, the term sound doctrine refers to the entire message of God and his plan to redeem sinners for himself through Jesus Christ.[27] Everything from who God is to Christ's second coming is all part of "sound doctrine." In other words, it is the message of eternal life in Christ Jesus. Paul puts "sound doctrine" in direct opposition to the false gospel of the "circumcision party" in Titus 1:9-10. The sound doctrines were the foundational and essential doctrines of our faith. This is the truth that Titus and the elders were to guard and teach with all of their might. Without this sound doctrine, there will be no true godliness in the lives of the church members. Only the true gospel can produce genuine godliness in our lives.

So one might ask, "If this sound doctrine leads to godliness, should I still teach people to be godly, or should I simply preach gospel doctrine and stay away from teaching on how Christians must behave in the world?" This first verse of chapter 2 gives us the answer.

❖ *What instructions does Paul give in Titus 2:1?*

---

[27] Notice these word from Spurgeon from his sermon "Preach the Gospel": To preach the gospel is to state every doctrine contained in God's Word, and to give every truth its proper prominence." (Spurgeon, The New Park Street Pulpit Vol.1&2, pg.262. 2007) The doctrines that Paul is discussing are not limited to the truth of the death, burial, and resurrection, although that is the actual act that purchased our salvation. I use the word *gospel* in the broader sense that Paul had in mind when he said "on that day when, according to my *gospel*, God judges the secrets of men by Christ Jesus." (Romans 2:16)

❖ *What do you think he means when he says "what accords with sound doctrine"?*

Paul says to "teach what accords with sound doctrine." In other words, Paul was telling Titus to teach them what godliness looks like and make the picture clear. There is to be no hesitation about what holiness looks like in a believer's life. However, this is not only for the believer's sake, but also for the unbeliever and the church as a whole. When the people are challenged to live godly lives and they know what that looks like, they will much more quickly recognize the false teacher who is living an ungodly life and seeking to lead them down the same sinful path. Jesus taught that we would know the false teachers by the fruit we see in their lives.[28] For this reason, we must be taught what the good fruit looks like and what the bad fruit looks like. A faithful preacher should give the false teacher and the false believer no place to hide his sin. In the end, the believer will be challenged to keep growing in his faith and dealing with his personal sin, while the unbeliever who does not intend to forsake his sin will be exposed.

However, as important as these things are, they are not the primary goal that Paul has in mind when he gives this instruction to Titus. In the following verses, notice the reasons that Paul gives us for godly living.

---

[28] Matthew 7:15-17 "Beware of false prophets, who come to you in sheep's clothing but inwardly are ravenous wolves. You will recognize them by their fruits. Are grapes gathered from thornbushes, or figs from thistles? So, every healthy tree bears good fruit, but the diseased tree bears bad fruit."

❖ *In verse 5, we find Paul instructing the women in godly character. Although Paul is instructing them in godly living, that is not his main concern. What is Paul's main concern in this verse?*

❖ *In verse 10, we find Paul addressing slaves and admonishing them to serve their masters well. What does their faithful service do for the doctrine of God?*

It should be evident by now that God cares deeply about how we live day to day. There is no better way to bear witness to the power of God and the gospel than to live in holiness. Yet this is a point on which we must be clear: our lives are not the gospel! Many people make the mistake of believing that they can *live* the gospel. They cannot! The gospel is not something *we* do, but rather something that God has done for us. When people see our good works, they do not see the gospel directly. They see the way the gospel has changed us, but they do not see the message of God's redemption in Christ unless we *tell them.*

❖ *Have you ever heard someone say that they do not know how to tell people about Christ, so they just share the gospel with the way they live their lives?*

❖ *The gospel simply means "good news." What do you think that people mean when they say they are witnessing or preaching the gospel with their lives?*

❖ *What might be a better way for a person to understand the good news of the gospel?*

When a believer lives a holy life, they are not preaching the gospel, they are making the gospel shine by acting in a way that shows its power and beauty. Either we will display the power of the gospel in our lives or we will live in a way that makes the gospel look powerless. God's plan is for us to make the gospel look glorious and powerful. Paul calls this *adorning* the gospel. The focus of this exhortation is on the glory of God and the gospel message. Our lives should constantly be directing people to Jesus Christ and the one message that can transform a sinner into a saint. This is so important that most of the book of Titus is taken up with this kind of teaching. Paul makes it very clear that there is a specific way that Christians are to live.

To make sure that we understand the way faith in the gospel and godliness fit together, let us notice the analogy that the Bible gives us.

What do the following verses tell us about God's Word? What is it compared to?

❖ *1 Peter 1:23*

❖ *Mark 4:14*

Now what are Biblical virtues and obedience compared to?

❖ *Galatians 5:22-23*

❖ *Romans 7:4*

This is a very understandable picture for us. The seed is God's Word and the fruit that grows out of this seed is our changed life.

❖ *In Luke 6:43-45 we see a great explanation of how this works. Where does good fruit come from?*

❖ *Where does bad fruit come from?*

As we all know, a good tree can only come from good seed (the gospel). This means that Titus was to do the opposite of what the false teachers had been doing. Their false teaching had produced a bad tree, if you will, and its ugly fruit was now showing in the church.

❖ *What does Colossians 2:23 tell us about the power of self-made religion?*

Paul does not deny that man-made religion looks wise. It can look and sound so good on the outside because it often mixes some truth with some error. But in the end we are left without the power to stop the indulgence of our flesh. Only the transforming power of God's grace can change the kind of person we are on the inside; no amount of rules or rituals can do it. "The fruit follow[s] the nature of the tree; and there is no way to change the nature of the fruit, but by changing the nature of the tree which brings it forth."[29]

This is why it is essential that a faithful church preach a life-transforming gospel. When people come to repent of the sinful lives that they have lived and they place their trust completely in Christ and his work on the cross for them they have passed from

---

[29] Owen, J. (1971). *The Holy Spirit.* Grand Rapids, MI: Sovereign Grace Publishers.p.223

death to life.[30] With their eyes on Christ, they now have the correct foundation for godly living and they will desire further instruction on how Christ intends for them to live in this world. These instructions are for those who are already believers, not directions for those who want to earn their way to heaven.

> Do not present your members to sin as instruments for unrighteousness, but present yourselves to God as those who have been brought from death to life, and your members to God as instruments for righteousness. For sin will have no dominion over you, since you are not under law but under grace. Romans 6:13-14

---

[30] John 5:24 Truly, truly, I say to you, whoever hears my word and believes him who sent me has eternal life. He does not come into judgment, but has passed from death to life.

Chapter 7

A Life that Adorns the Gospel

> [2]Older men are to be sober-minded, dignified, self-controlled, sound in faith, in love, and in steadfastness. [3]Older women likewise are to be reverent in behavior, not slanderers or slaves to much wine. They are to teach what is good, [4] and so train the young women to love their husbands and children, [5]to be self-controlled, pure, working at home, kind, and submissive to their own husbands. [6]Likewise, urge the younger men to be self-controlled. [7]Show yourself in all respects to be a model of good works, and in your teaching show integrity, dignity, [8]and sound speech that cannot be condemned, so that an opponent may be put to shame, having nothing evil to say about us. [9]Slaves are to be submissive to their own masters in everything; they are to be well-pleasing, not argumentative, [10]not pilfering, but showing all good faith, so that in everything they may adorn the doctrine of God our Savior. Titus 2:1-10

This text of Scripture is a brief example of the teaching that "accords with sound doctrine." This is the kind of teaching that must be present in a healthy church that believes the gospel. As 1Timothy 1:5 says, the very aim of the gospel charge is a transformed life.[31] God's desire is for his people to bear good fruit that brings honor to his name and to the power of his gospel. In this chapter, we will look at this sample of godly instruction so that we might follow in Titus' footsteps as he sought to build a healthy church.

Older Men (Titus 2:2)

Here Paul begins his description of the gospel-centered man. He begins with the "older man." We see that the man of God must be "sober-minded." It has the idea of being clear-headed and refraining from excess. How easy it is for a man to drift into excess! Yet a godly man is clear-headed and waiting for his master's return (1 Peter 1:13[32]).

Paul also instructs the older men to be "dignified." The word has the idea of being serious and honorable in his attitude toward life. The godly man should not be careless in his approach to life. This serious and honorable attitude is cultivated by the fear of the Lord. Of all Christians, older men should be an example of dignity in the fear of God.

In addition, a man with a truly dignified character must also display self control. According to Titus 1:12, the culture they lived in was anything but self-controlled. What better way for a man to display Christian character than to be self-controlled? As godly men, there was to be a vast difference between them and the world they lived in.

Finally, we find another reference to "soundness." We find that the godly man must be sound in his faith, in his love, and in his steadfastness. These three virtues also appear together in 1

---

[31] 1Timothy 1:5 "The aim of our charge is love that issues from a pure heart and a good conscience and a sincere faith. "

[32] 1Peter 1:13 "Therefore, preparing your minds for action, and being sober-minded, set your hope fully on the grace that will be brought to you at the revelation of Jesus Christ."

Thessalonians 1:2-3[33] and they seem to be a summary of the basic attitude of a believer. Each of these virtues is a direct response to the gospel message. A sound faith refers to our trust in Christ and his work on the cross. A sound love describes our relationship to the wonderful Savior that we have come to trust. Moreover, steadfastness describes our ability to stand firm through trials because we have such a great and glorious hope. These virtues are all found within the heart of the man, yet each one leads to obvious changes in his behavior. This is always the way God works through the gospel. The transformation of life takes place in the heart of the believer and works its way out into a changed life. A healthy church needs older men who have walked with God and will be able to bear witness to the transforming power of God in their lives.

Older Women (Titus 2:3-4)

Next, we find Paul's instruction for godly womanhood. We will notice that Paul addresses the older and then the younger women, so that we gain one beautiful picture of godly womanhood. Throughout the Scripture, we learn that women hold a vital place in God's plan for both the family and the church. In these verses, we find a brief description of this high calling for the women of God in our midst.

Paul begins by instructing the older women to be "reverent" in their behavior. The word "reverent" refers to "being suited to a sacred character." A godly woman will stand out in the world and the church when her actions reflect an inward character that is set apart to God. This exhortation reminds us that our actions must match our profession. A woman of God does not stand out for what she *says* she believes, but for what she *shows* she believes.

---

[33] 1Thessalonians 1:2-3 "We give thanks to God always for all of you, constantly mentioning you in our prayers, remembering before our God and Father your work of faith and labor of love and steadfastness of hope in our Lord Jesus Christ."

Then we notice that they are not to be slanderers. This is a common theme in the New Testament and points to a dangerous pitfall for many people. A slanderer is someone who makes false accusations about another person and thus tears down that person's character. Slander often accompanies gossip and is a very serious sin to God. In fact, this is the term used 34 times in the New Testament for Satan himself. He is the "Slanderer."

The women were also to be free from slavery to wine. It is not surprising to find an exhortation like this given to those on the island of Crete based on what we have already learned. The Scriptures make it very clear that slavery to wine (or drunkenness) is the opposite of godly virtue, since it removes even the natural self-control that an unbeliever normally exercises. Paul tells us in Ephesians 5:18, "and do not get drunk with wine, for that is debauchery, but be filled with the Spirit." In the place of this debauchery, God calls the older women of the church to be filled with the Spirit so that their lives will be under his control.

The Ministry of the Mature

Tucked inside this chapter on holy living we also find some very important direction for ministry in the local church. In these simple verses, we discover the vital role that godly, mature women play in the life of a healthy church. If we have been around good teaching for very long it is easy to simply pass through a passage like this and assume that we already have a sufficient grasp of these "basics." While we might very well understand the general concepts (since God has kept the truth very simple for us), this does not necessarily mean we are obeying them. This passage presents us with a pattern that churches commonly neglect or simply overlook to their own loss.

❖ *According to Titus 2:3-4, what two words does Paul use to describe the older women's duty to the younger women?*

❖ *Is this a pattern that you normally see in the local church (yours or those around you)?*

Paul says that the older women are to *teach* what is good and so *train* the young women. While this seems to be a neglected pattern in many churches today, it is packed with practical wisdom. If the older women are not teaching the younger women about raising a family, who will? Titus and the elders could clearly lay out the Scripture's teaching on womanhood, but they could never be a model or an example to the younger women in these areas.

Not only that, but this pattern also preserves the purity and testimony of the church. Sadly, it is a shameful reality that men in ministry often fall into temptation and sexual sin as a result of "ministering" to (or closely with) a woman in the church. Notice how simply that issue is completely removed when the older women fulfill this responsibility. The older women are to teach the younger women how to live out the gospel at home. When Paul adds the word train to his instruction, it becomes clear that this is a primary means of discipleship for young women.

With all the emphasis on elders, one might assume that the elders would handle all of the teaching in the church. It is true that the elders bear the responsibility to teach, lead, and guard the flock of God. What we see here, though, is the effect of faithful leadership by the elders. The flock is not to be passively receiving the Word, but actively living out the Word in such a way as to affect those around them.

As the elders lead the people, the people should in turn lead others by example and teaching. This does not refer exclusively to those who are older in age but to those who are older in the faith. We know this because the younger Titus was to lead the "older men." Hence we see, this is not simply a pattern for women but the men as well. This wonderful section on godly living does not leave us without direction for fulfilling the Great Commission. Rather it gives simple, straightforward instructions that can and should be put into practice by every believer as they reach maturity in their faith.

Younger Women (Titus 2:4-5)

So what are the older women supposed to model and teach to the young women? They are to teach them to "love their husbands and children." While this is a very simple concept, it is not always easy to love biblically. This is not talking about warm fuzzy feelings. It refers to the sacrificial love that Christ taught his disciples. We find a wonderful summary in 1 Corinthians 13 and a perfect example in the life of Christ. There we see what God means when he tells us to love. The younger women need examples that can do more than explain the concept of godliness. What younger women (or men) need is to be able to see someone older in their faith who actually does these things. This also implies that the older women were mature in these areas. From their own struggles and growth in the Lord, older people can give practical wisdom that only experience can bring.

Next, we see that godly womanhood involves self-control. This word is also translated "sensible" in some Bible versions. This is the only quality that Paul mentions for each group of people in the church.

Thirdly, we find that the young women were to learn to keep their homes in order. Paul says that they are to be "working at home." This clearly teaches that God has ordained for women who have families to make the home the focus of their service to God. It is too easy for other things (including competition with the husband) to become a distraction and a misplaced priority. From the biblical example of the Proverbs 31 woman, we see that this does not mean a woman cannot work outside the home, but it does mean that she is to see the care of the home as *her God-given responsibility*. In our day, people do not honor motherhood as God intended. In fact, many who read this passage could see it as demeaning and/or insulting. We must recover the honor of motherhood in our churches and demonstrate it in our homes.

❖ *Read Proverbs 31:10-31. What kind of work are verses 14, 16, and 24 referring to? Is it inside or outside the home?*

❖ *What is her attitude towards her husband? (v.12)*

❖ *What is her attitude towards her children? What does she do for them? (vv. 15 and 27)*

❖ *When she works outside the home, why does she do it? Is it for personal ambition and self-fulfillment, or is it to honor her husband and care for her household?*

The Proverbs 31 woman provides the perfect example for godly womanhood. She is industrious and hardworking, yet she does not neglect her family in pursuit of other worldly dreams. Instead, she recognizes the honor and responsibility of motherhood and she devotes herself to it with joy. She is an example of what Paul refers to when he says that women are to be "working at home."

Finally, Paul tells Titus that the young women are to be kind and submissive to their own husbands. Our culture, and many in the church today, do not accept this teaching. We must understand that this is not a side issue. Paul specifically chose to address this issue for a good reason. He could have skipped it, but he did not because marriage is a picture of the believer's relationship to God.

❖ *In Ephesians 5:22-24 we find the Biblical foundation for submission. How are the husband and wife to relate to each other?*

❖ *What does it reflect to the world?*

This concept comes directly out of the nature of God himself. The Scriptures teach that God the Son (Jesus Christ) is in perfect obedience to God the Father.[34] The same is true of the Holy Spirit.[35] This does not mean that they are inferior to the Father or that the Father is harsh or unkind to the Son. God is an example of perfect unity, equality, and submission. This may be a new thought to some, but it is vital for the testimony of the gospel that we live out this command.

Young Men (Titus 2:6-8)

In verse 6, we come to the very short exhortation to young men. Paul simply tells them to be self-controlled. Paul has emphasized this character trait for every group so far. In doing this, he seems to use this one trait to summarize Christian behavior in the world. In light of the wicked culture that surrounded them, this would probably be the most obvious difference between those who belonged to Christ and those who did not. This seems to be Peter's point as he addresses believers in 1 Peter 4:1-5:

Since therefore Christ suffered in the flesh, arm yourselves with the same way of thinking, for whoever has suffered in the flesh has ceased from sin, so as to live for the rest of the time in the flesh no longer for human passions but for the will of God. For the time that is past suffices for doing what the Gentiles want to do, living in sensuality, passions, drunkenness, orgies, drinking parties, and lawless idolatry. With respect to this they are surprised when you do not join them in the same flood of debauchery, and they malign you; but they will give account to him who is ready to judge the living and the dead.

---

[34] Hebrews 5:8 "Although he was a son, he learned obedience through what he suffered."

[35] John 14:26 "But the Helper, the Holy Spirit, whom the Father will send in my name, he will teach you all things and bring to your remembrance all that I have said to you."

This self-control reflects a heart that is consumed with the gospel. With their minds set on Christ, these young men would learn to think as he did. Young men must think of themselves as those who have died to the sin in which they once lived. As Peter says, it will cause others to mock, but he reminds them of the final outcome – "they will give an account to him who is ready to judge the living and the dead!" The wide path that this world follows always leads to destruction. In the face of temptations, the young man must keep his eyes on Christ and the tremendous promises that believers have. It is this hope that will carry him on to the end.

In the other details of life, the young men should follow the example of the overseers and the older men in the church. As we have seen, this is a God ordained pattern of ministry and discipleship in the church.

Paul then moves from the young men in general and speaks to Titus, who must have been a younger man himself. It seems to makes sense, if he is a younger man, to speak to him when addressing the other young men. As a leader and a younger man, he had a special responsibility that rested upon him. Paul tells him to be a model both of good works and of integrity in teaching. As we have already seen, there is nothing more important than faithful teaching. As Titus confronted the false teachers, appointed elders, and set things in order, there would surely be opposition. Titus had to be above reproach so that there was no legitimate way that they could discredit the true gospel ministry.

The Slaves (Titus 2:9-10)

Finally, Paul addresses the last group that was often found in first century households: slaves. These were men, women, and children who were owned and completely subject to their masters. Sometimes they were treated with dignity and well cared for. Other times, they were treated no better than the livestock, often performing the most menial of tasks. While slavery does not exist in our society, these verses carry a lot of practical instruction for us.

First, we can see the radical message of the gospel, as it transformed even the slave/master relationship of the first century. The gospel caused people who were slaves of men yet free from their sin (1 Corinthians 7:22)[36] to love and serve with a motivation beyond what the lost world could understand.

Second, we see a practical application for all who work under an employer. If God expects this kind of service for a master who may or may not be cruel, then what must he expect of those who are paid to do their work?

We see a very clear instruction for the slaves to be submissive in everything. Paul teaches the principle of submitting to one's master in Ephesians 6:5-8.

❖ *What is the attitude God requires?*

❖ *What is the kind of service that God condemns?*

---

[36] 1Corinthians 7:22 "For he who was called in the Lord as a slave is a freedman of the Lord. Likewise he who was free when called is a slave of Christ."

❖ *As we render service to earthly men, who is our ultimate allegiance to?*

❖ *Who are we looking for a reward from?*

This requires a completely different view of the world. The only truth that sets men free to love and serve in this way is the gospel. Only those who know that they have been freed from bondage far worse than earthly slavery could live and act in this way. In living this way, the believers would "adorn" the truth of the gospel. This means that they would live a life that brings honor to the truth. They do this by putting their freedom in Christ on display by good works.

> For this is the will of God, that by doing good you should put to silence the ignorance of foolish people. Live as people who are free, not using your freedom as a cover-up for evil, but living as servants of God. 1 Peter 2:15-16

Chapter 8

Grace: the Power of Gospel-Centered Living

> [11]*For the grace of God has appeared, bringing salvation for all people,* [12]*training us to renounce ungodliness and worldly passions, and to live self-controlled, upright, and godly lives in the present age,* [13]*waiting for our blessed hope, the appearing of the glory of our great God and Savior Jesus Christ,* [14]*who gave himself for us to redeem us from all lawlessness and to purify for himself a people for his own possession who are zealous for good works.* [15]*Declare these things; exhort and rebuke with all authority. Let no one disregard you. Titus 2:11-15*

The standards are high! For a person with a worldly outlook on life, these commands can be confusing or even offensive. This is why we must understand that the gospel is central to everything else in life. If a person rejects the truths of the gospel, they have rejected the foundation of godly living. To try to build a godly life apart from the gospel is like trying to build a house without a foundation. It cannot be done.

As we come to Titus 2:11-15, we find Paul reminding the believers of the great gospel foundation that they have.

The Grace of God *at Work*

Titus 2:11 begins a section of Scripture that is all about the transforming work of God in our lives. Everything in this passage can be traced back to one word in this verse.

❖ *What has appeared, according to Titus 2:11?*

❖ *What has grace brought?*

❖ *What does grace do in Titus 2:12?*

This is a very important concept for us to understand. Many see this passage as saying, "God has been so kind to you that it makes you feel like being kind too." While that surely should be true, it is missing the main point. It is not simply saying that I am so thankful for grace that I figure out how to live better myself. It is saying that the grace of God is *at work* in us. The word "training" is a very active word. It refers to training a child when he is young, and it carries the idea of discipline and punishment as well. It is active and alive in us. It is powerful!

❖ *Have you ever thought of grace in this way? Read Hebrews 12:5-8. What does it tell us about how God treats those who are his sons?*

❖ *What does it say about those who receive no training or discipline from God?*

In these verses, we see the way God deals with those who are his children. It is God's grace that does both the saving and the training in righteousness. In the Hebrews passage, we see that those without this discipline are not God's true children. This is the same as saying that they have *no grace.*

Titus was to teach the things that accord with sound doctrine, but not in a way that left people looking to themselves for strength. God's grace in Christ is the source of the training. As we saw in Hebrews 12, God disciplines his children whether or not they ask or even understand what he is doing. It is God at work for the good of the believer, whether he understands it all or not.

❖ *Paul was a perfect living example of the power of God's grace. According to 1 Corinthians 15:9-10, what changed Paul from persecutor to an apostle?*

❖ *What was it that caused Paul to work harder than any of the other apostles?*

It is important to notice that the things that God's grace trains us to do are exactly the same things that Titus was teaching this church to do. Therefore, Titus was to teach a gospel of grace; this was his "sound doctrine." Yet this gospel would begin to transform those who believed. The power of grace would be in them and would begin to train them. When Titus taught on godly character, he was simply working with God's grace. Titus became a tool in the hands of God.

The Grace of God *Yet to Come*

Titus 2:13 takes this a step further. God's grace was also training them to look for a promise that was yet to come.

❖ *Read Titus 2:13. What does grace teach us to do in this verse?*

❖ *What is our blessed hope? What are we looking for?*

This is a wonderful, yet deeply challenging verse. Notice that this verse does not say we are looking for heaven or a reunion with our loved ones who have died. It says we are looking for "the glorious appearing of our great God and Savior Jesus Christ." This love for Christ is a wonderful evidence of true faith.

To comfort Christians who may be weak in their faith, J. C. Ryle said the following:

> For one thing, if you love Christ in deed and truth, rejoice in the thought that you have good evidence about the state of your soul. Love, I tell you this day, is an evidence of grace.[37]

Are we growing to love him in a way that stirs this longing to see him? Paul does not say that we love him as much as we should, because we are still in "training." Every believer has much further to grow in his walk with Christ than he knows. However, if God's grace is in him, he will love Christ.[38]

Notice what the following verses teach us about the effect of this glorious hope:

❖ *1 Peter 1:13 – According to this verse, what attitude or mindset are we to have as we wait for our great hope?*

❖ *1 John 3:3 - How does this hope affect us in our day-to-day struggle with sin?*

---

[37] Ryle, J. C. (2010). *Holiness: Its Nature, Hindrances, Difficulties, and Roots* . (Location 4793) Unknown, Kindle Edition.

[38] 1 Corinthians 16:22 "If anyone has no love for the Lord, let him be accursed. Our Lord, come!"

❖ *Based on these verses, would you say that our hope is a side issue?*

❖ *Would you say that your hope is in the right place?*

Titus 2:13 makes it clear that believers are to look for Christ. Grace makes Christ, not our works, the focus of our hope. We look to *him* and for *him*.

The Grace of God Frees Us to Serve

This truth continues in Titus 2:14. Here we find the goal that Christ had in mind when he came to the cross for us. This is a very important point for us to consider.

❖ *What was Christ's purpose in giving himself for us, according to Titus 2:14?*

This truth has a huge impact on our view of salvation. When we consider the freeness of God's mercy and the completeness of our forgiveness, it is too easy to assume that sin is a small and trifling problem in our lives. In fact, it is this very concept that has opened the door for many false teachers to enter the church and teach that we are free to live any way we want. Often they do not say it this bluntly, but it is the substance of their teaching. They will find many ways to tickle the ears of their hearers; however, they do not teach men and women to adorn the gospel with good works as Paul is telling Titus to do. The pattern of living that Titus 2 gives us fits with Christ's purpose in redeeming us from all lawlessness.

> ❖ *The word for redeem means to release by paying a ransom. What did Jesus redeem us from?*

This truth must shape our understanding of salvation. We are not saved *to* sin, but *from* sin. The picture of redemption is a picture of freedom from slavery. Before salvation, we were in bondage to this lawlessness with no hope of freedom. In order to appreciate the magnitude of our salvation, we must understand that we have been freed from lawlessness. Although the Scriptures consistently teach this truth, humanity will often seek a more pleasant view of itself. We are surrounded by a world that desperately wants to find goodness in mankind. Because of this, the world is constantly telling us that mankind is basically good, with a few "hang-ups" here and there. Nevertheless, the Scripture is unflinching in its declaration that all men are in slavery to Satan himself, who the Bible calls the "god of this world."[39] This means that we were part of the kingdom of darkness before our conversion and enemies of God; therefore, we faced God's

---

[39] 2 Corinthians 4:4 "In their case the god of this world has blinded the minds of the unbelievers, to keep them from seeing the light of the gospel of the glory of Christ, who is the image of God."

punishment for our sins. However, God has now freed all believers from this captivity, and transferred them into Christ's own kingdom. The just punishment for our rebellion was laid upon Christ so that the rebels could be forgiven and freely received into his kingdom. This is the glorious message of Colossians 1:13-14:

> He has delivered us from the domain of darkness and transferred us to the kingdom of his beloved Son, in whom we have redemption, the forgiveness of sins.

❖ *According to Titus 2:14, who do we belong to now?*

Possession clearly indicates Christ's ownership. The language here is very special and conveys the idea of a treasured possession. Although we were sinful and disgusting to him before we were redeemed, he plans to purify his people so that they live and act in a way that is worthy of him. The goal is to have a people who look like their wonderful Master.

This brings up an implication that many people miss. Many people think of themselves as free beings who do what they want. In fact, this attitude is almost universal among unbelievers. They refuse to give up their "freedom" in order to obey God. They want to do what they want to do. What they do not realize is that every person outside of Christ is a part of the kingdom of darkness. Their rebellion against God simply proves that they serve their master (Satan) very well.

❖ *According to Titus 2:14, can we be free from Satan without belonging to God? Is there ever a time where a person is his or her own master?*

Our rebellion against this idea of belonging to God and owing him our obedience comes from sin. In fact, this is the essence of the very first sin ever committed. In Genesis 3:5-6, we see that the essence of the first temptation and the first sin was the desire to be like God. This desire is still with us today. Believers must remember that God's work to make us obedient children is not completed. Grace is still at work in believers because there is still much training to be done. If we forget this, we could despair when we see how much sin we still struggle with. That is why our eyes must be set upon God's grace and not our performance. In Christ, we find both the forgiveness we need and the grace to become pure in our day-to-day lives. May we keep our eyes on grace and not on ourselves. This is where our fruit comes from.

❖ *Finally, we see what the outward fruit is to be. According to Titus 2:14, what does God want his people to be known for?*

The theme of good works fills this little book of Titus. We see that good works is one of the outward fruits of God's grace in our lives. It is the way that Christ's servants live. Obviously, this teaching could be unpopular in a culture as lazy and ungodly as Crete.

❖ *Notice the way that Paul commands Titus to go about this work in Titus 2:15. What is Titus instructed to do in this verse?*

This puts an exclamation point on this powerful passage. Titus was to teach a gospel of transforming grace and a glorious hope. As we see in this closing verse, this was always Paul's message.

> But now that you have been set free from sin and have become slaves of God, the fruit you get leads to sanctification and its end, eternal life. Romans 6:22

Chapter 9

Teach Gospel-Centered Living in the World

> *¹Remind them to be submissive to rulers and authorities, to be obedient, to be ready for every good work, ²to speak evil of no one, to avoid quarreling, to be gentle, and to show perfect courtesy toward all people. ³For we ourselves were once foolish, disobedient, led astray, slaves to various passions and pleasures, passing our days in malice and envy, hated by others and hating one another. Titus 3:1-3*

In this chapter, we find Paul resuming his practical instruction for adorning sound doctrine. He has just paused to remind them of the power of the gospel and now he turns to another part of daily life where the gospel must be applied. Instead of addressing the various members of the church, he now addresses the church as a whole and tells them how God wants them to relate to the world.

This passage is not for those who simply call themselves believers yet continue to live like the world. This passage is for those who understand that Christ has called them to be holy and separate from the world. They embrace the calling to be Christ's own possession and they live differently as they wait for him to return. These are the people who need to know how to relate to the world and its systems. For instance, how does a person who truly embraces Christ as the King of all kings relate to their earthly king? Moreover, how do we relate to those who are still in bondage to sin? Do we love them, hate them, or just avoid them? Throughout history, professing Christians have done horrible things in the name of Christ. Many of these atrocities could have been avoided had they understood the truth of the gospel and how Christ intends for believers to live in this world.

❖ *Does verse 1 of chapter 3 tell us that they already knew these things, or does he imply that this idea was new to them?*

This means that they had already been taught these things, but they were in danger of forgetting or forsaking them.

Obey Civil Authorities

❖ *What kind of **attitude** does Paul command toward "rulers and authorities" in Titus 3:1?*

❖ *We know that Crete had a reputation for ungodliness and corruption. Do you think this would have been an easy or difficult command? Why?*

This is an essential truth for Christians to understand. God demands a submissive attitude towards those who are in positions of worldly authority. Christians are especially vulnerable to grumbling and complaining when it comes to dealing with earthly governments. This is because Christians, of all people, would be most grieved by their ungodliness. Yet this easily crosses the line into a self-righteous attitude. How many times have Christians made the rulers of their country the target of their jokes and sarcasm? Here, Paul condemns this as wrong.

❖ *What kind of works are they to display in relation to the rulers and authorities?*

While this may seem difficult, we need to remember that this is about adorning the doctrine of God our Savior. We must never let our freedom in Christ be an excuse for acting in a way that would bring disgrace upon the gospel we proclaim.

In the area of submitting to rulers, we must remember that we ultimately serve Christ, and his command is to be obedient to our rulers and do good works. Since this is an important, yet complicated issue for the church, we will spend a little extra time looking through some other passages so that we understand this clearly.

❖ *Notice what 1 Peter 2:13-17 teaches about submission to authorities. Who does Peter say we should be in submission to?*

❖ *What is the purpose of our obedience in verse 15?*

❖ *In verse 16, we learn that we have freedom from the world as believers. Does this truth mean that we do not submit to the government or that we must submit to the government even more?*

❖ *In Romans 13:1-7, we find some very important theological principles. What do verses 1-2 teach us about governing authorities?*

❖ *What does verse 4 tell us about God's purpose in establishing governments?*

❖ *What is the extent of our required obedience in verse 7?*

Does this mean that everything the government does is good? To answer this, all we have to do is follow the history of the Old Testament. It is obvious that the governments were not always obedient to God in all things. Much of the Old Testament is the sad account of God's judgment upon wicked nations. However, we also see who it is that raised up kings and brought them down. It was God. Even as God's people were carried off to pagan Babylon because of their sin, we find that the godly were instructed to seek the good of that pagan kingdom (Jeremiah 29:4-7).[40] Daniel served multiple pagan kings with great faithfulness; however, he did not dishonor God in the process. The only time he neglected a law was when it told him not to pray to his God, and that was a setup! God intends for us to obey those who are in authority, even when they are known for great sin. Just take the world Paul lived in as an example. Who was it that crucified Christ and persecuted believers? It was the government. Yet God accomplished his predetermined plan through those events.[41] What if Jesus had gathered an army and fought back? What if there had been no persecution to scatter the believers who then carried the gospel to other nations?

❖ *What does Paul urge the godly to do for their governments in 1 Timothy 2:1-4?*

---

[40] Jeremiah 29:7 "But seek the welfare of the city where I have sent you into exile, and pray to the LORD on its behalf, for in its welfare you will find your welfare."

[41] Acts 2:23 "This Jesus, delivered up according to the definite plan and foreknowledge of God, you crucified and killed by the hands of lawless men."

❖   *Why is this pleasing to God? (v.4)*

There are always questions about whether we should obey the government even if it commands something that is against God's law. What do the following passages teach us?

❖   *Daniel 3:14-18*

❖   *Acts 4:13-20*

There is one question of extreme importance to the believer: is Christ's kingdom an earthly kingdom that competes with other earthly kingdoms or is it a heavenly kingdom that will only be revealed when Christ returns?

❖   *What does Jesus tell Pilate in John 18:36?*

❖ *What does Jesus say we would do if the kingdom were of this world?*

❖ *What does this tell us about mixing the church with the kingdoms of this world?*

We must understand this truth. Far too many have sought to spread the "gospel" by war and have used the church for political ends. Certainly, there are certain moral and ethical demands upon a believer and these will affect his life as a citizen. However, we should never see the church as an earthly kingdom. The church is part of a heavenly kingdom that will only be established when the King returns. May we be satisfied with that promise and not grasp for earthly power in the name of Christ.

I hope that these passages have given us a clear picture of what God requires of the church in relation to earthly rulers. May we apply these truths and be submissive to our rulers and authorities, remaining obedient, and ready for every good work.

Speak and Act for the Gospel

Having seen our proper relationship to the governments of this world, we now turn to how we conduct ourselves among the people of this world in general.

❖ *According to Titus 3:2, what is our first command in relating to the ungodly?*

This could be directed towards our rulers as well as our neighbors. Either way, we see that our speech is to be pure and kind. Here Paul addresses the temptation for believers to be self-righteous in their dealings with the ungodly.

❖ *What are we supposed to avoid according to this same verse?*

❖ *Why do you think that he warns against quarreling?*

As witnesses of Christ who proclaim the gospel, we often encounter a hostile response from the world. Often our message is labeled foolish or offensive. The natural reaction could be to quarrel with the lost over these issues. We could even feel like our quarreling is "defending the faith." Yet this verse reminds us that quarreling does not adorn the gospel we are preaching. We should be bold, but not quarrelsome.

Notice how the following verses connect our conduct among the lost and our witness for Christ.

❖ *In Colossians 4:6, we find God's will for our speech. What does God want our speech to be like? Why?*

❖ *According to 1 Peter 3:15-16, what should we be prepared to talk about?*

❖ *What kind of speech are we to use?*

Our speech is one of the most powerful tools we have in our proclamation of the gospel, but maybe in a different way than we think. The tongue is extremely powerful, and if we let it loose in sinful talk, it will do great harm to the cause of Christ and the testimony of the church.

❖ *On the positive side, what godly character traits must we show toward the lost? (Titus 3:2)*

The first of these is translated "gentle" in the ESV. The Greek word is *epieikēs*. Literally, the word means fitting or appropriate. In this case, it refers to a gentle, patient way of dealing with the people of the world. As we read this, we must keep our worldly setting in mind. This gentleness is to be shown in the face of the world's mocking and persecution.

Finally, we are told to show "perfect courtesy toward all people." Some translations use the word meekness to describe this godly attitude. The Greek word here is *praotēs*, and refers to a humble, submissive inward attitude. While the word gentle points to our dealings with others, perfect courtesy describes an inward attitude. In these two exhortations, we see that we are to have a genuine inward courtesy as well as an outward gentleness.

These are the attitudes that adorn the gospel. By showing gentleness and perfect courtesy, we are reflecting our Savior's attitude toward us (Phil. 2:4-8). He displayed perfect selflessness and humility when he chose to bear our sins on the cross. The world needs to see that reflected in us as we preach this gospel.

> *Have this mind among yourselves, which is yours in Christ Jesus, who, though he was in the form of God, did not count equality with God a thing to be grasped, but made himself nothing, taking the form of a servant, being born in the likeness of men. And being found in human form, he humbled himself by becoming obedient to the point of death, even death on a cross.*
> *Philippians 2:5-8*

Chapter 10

A Life Based on Gospel Mercy

> *³For we ourselves were once foolish, disobedient, led astray, slaves to various passions and pleasures, passing our days in malice and envy, hated by others and hating one another. ⁴But when the goodness and loving kindness of God our Savior appeared, ⁵he saved us, not because of works done by us in righteousness, but according to his own mercy, by the washing of regeneration and renewal of the Holy Spirit, ⁶whom he poured out on us richly through Jesus Christ our Savior, ⁷so that being justified by his grace we might become heirs according to the hope of eternal life. ⁸The saying is trustworthy, and I want you to insist on these things, so that those who have believed in God may be careful to devote themselves to good works. These things are good and profitable for all people. Titus 3:3-8*

In chapter 9 of this study, we learned how Christians must treat their government as well as those who do not believe the gospel. As Paul is writing to Titus and this young church, he realizes how difficult this instruction may be. He has already faced a great amount of personal suffering for his bold proclamation of the gospel. In fact, Paul himself warned, "All who desire to live a godly life in Christ Jesus will be persecuted."[42] It is one thing to be patient when others mock you for your faith; it is another to be patient when they burn your house or beat you.

What motivation does Paul give believers in light of the real hardships they would face as witnesses of Christ? He brings them back to the gospel!

❖ *How does Paul describe these believers (and us) in Titus 3:3?*

The first thing that we notice in this verse is the reminder of every believer's past. As bad as unbelievers may appear to be, we must remember that we were all in the same position at one time. Here Paul paints a vivid picture of our own sin and its deadly effects. This is intended to remind every believer of the time when he was dead in his sin and separated from all hope.

However, we learn more than sympathy from these verses, we also learn how far God reached down to save us. Understanding the true state of a lost person is foundational to understanding the gospel correctly. We must understand the sickness correctly to understand the type of cure that is needed. For a minor injury, you only need a minor cure. For a massive injury, you need a tremendous cure. Many today believe in the basic goodness of man. They see sin as a superficial problem and tend to treat sin as a mere "mistake." In this case, salvation is seen as re-education. The basically good person needs to learn how to express the

---

[42] 2 Timothy 3:12

goodness of his heart and avoid the bad influences around him. Is this the picture that Paul is painting?

A Portrait of a Lost Man

The first word that Paul uses to describe the lost person is "foolish." This refers to a foolishness, or lack of wisdom, in the things of God. As we saw in chapter 3 of this study, the lost person thinks the gospel is a foolish message. They do not see the seriousness of their danger and they often mock or simply ignore the message of salvation in Christ because they are foolish about the things of God

Not only are they foolish about divine things, but they are disobedient. The Bible clearly teaches that this is the universal attitude of the unconverted. He has a natural bent to rebel against God and disobey his commands.

❖ *Look up 1 Corinthians 2:12-14. How do we come to understand the things of God according to verse 12?*

❖ *What does verse 14 tell us about the natural man?*

Next, Paul reminds us that the lost are "led astray." This teaches us that lost people are actively being led away from God and his truth. They are deceived by the great deceiver himself, and the path they all walk is the broad road to destruction.[43]

❖ *In Ephesians 2:1-2, we find a passage that is very similar to our text in Titus. According to verse 2, who are we following as we are led astray?*

Unbelievers are also slaves to their passions and pleasures. This may sound like a mere figure of speech at first, but we will see that the Scriptures have much to say about this reality.[44]

❖ *What do John 8:34 and 44 say about those who practice sin?*

Finally, we see that sin taints all of our relationships. We pass our days in malice, envy, and hatred. Thankfully, God's grace keeps us from being as bad as we could be; nevertheless, our hearts are prone to all kinds of selfish desires that put us at odds

---

[43] Matthew 7:13-14 "Enter by the narrow gate. For the gate is wide and the way is easy that leads to destruction, and those who enter by it are many. For the gate is narrow and the way is hard that leads to life, and those who find it are few."

[44] Romans 6:17 "But thanks be to God, that you who were once slaves of sin have become obedient from the heart to the standard of teaching to which you were committed."

with others. This is simply the natural way of life for those who are slaves of sin.

This is not a very flattering picture of the human race, but it is exactly why God sent us a Savior. This is not a superficial problem, and the solution that God provided only drives this point home further.

❖ *Now Paul turns to a truth even more humbling than that. According to Titus 3:4, where does our salvation begin?*

❖ *According to Titus 3:5, what is the only reason for our salvation?*

❖ *Did our works or "righteous" character play any part at all?*

These verses are some of the most humbling verses in the Bible. First, we see what our character looked like to God. Then we see that our salvation and change of life was entirely God's work. There is not the smallest hint of our "goodness" or effort in these verses. It is God's mercy from beginning to end. This is why Paul refers to God as "God our Savior." Our God is a saving God!

❖ *Do these truths give us any reason at all to look down on others?*

❖ *What do you think our attitude toward the lost should be?*

It is important to notice that this description is in the past tense for those who are believers. This is a clear testimony to the fact that those who are truly saved have also been transformed. They are no longer what they once were. We know that this young church had many struggles and that there was still much to be put in order, yet these verses also teach us that there had been a genuine repentance. The evidence was that they *were* "once foolish...etc." As we saw in Titus 2:11, grace is a powerful force in the life of the believer. Now in Titus 3:5-6, we will see just how powerful God's grace is and what it accomplishes.

❖ *How does Titus 3:5-6 describe God's transforming work in our lives?*

Regeneration

In these verses, we come across a very important word that we all need to understand. This word is "regeneration." The word regeneration describes a new birth. So what does that mean and how does it relate to us as believers? As we have just seen, all mankind is born into slavery to sin. Our hearts and lives are ruled by it. Regeneration refers to a radical work of God the Holy Spirit who actually changes who we are in our innermost being. It is a real *change of heart* and it comes from God's mercy alone. Just as we were born the first time with an evil heart, Jesus taught that we must be born again to enter heaven. This means that our hearts must be transformed from hearts that love sin to hearts that love righteousness.

❖ *Read John 3:3-7. According to John 3:3, what does it take to get to heaven?*

❖ *What does verse 6 tell us about the source of this new birth?*

This verse explains what it means when Jesus says we must be born again. It is not another physical birth, but rather a spiritual birth. In the same way that our physical birth brought us physical life, our spiritual birth gives us spiritual life. Without this new spiritual life, we are nothing more than sinners who love our sin. As we have seen, every person who is born into this world is born with a sinful heart that is unable to please God or enter heaven.

This rebirth is the work of God to change our inner person. We begin to hunger for the things of God instead of the things of the world in the same way that a newborn baby hungers for milk. This change will one day be complete when we receive our resurrected bodies. Until that day, we will continue to struggle with our old sinfulness in these bodies of flesh.[45]

In Ezekiel 36:25-27, we find an amazing prophecy that describes this radical transformation that Jesus called the new birth.

❖ *According to verse 25, how was God going to cleanse his people?*

❖ *How does Titus 3:5 refer to this washing?*

❖ *According to Ezekiel 36:26, what was God going to do with his people's heart?*

---

[45] Galatians 5:17 "For the desires of the flesh are against the Spirit, and the desires of the Spirit are against the flesh, for these are opposed to each other, to keep you from doing the things you want to do."

❖ *How does Titus 3:5 refer to this change?*

This is no small work! According to these verses, regeneration is the complete transformation of a person's heart (or inner man). We see a beautiful connection between Titus 3:5-6 and Ezekiel 36:25-27.

Justification

The second term we must understand is "justification." Justification is a legal term that refers to a person being declared righteous in the sight of the law. While regeneration is a change that takes place in us, justification is not. Justification is about how God treats us. Instead of being punished for our sins against God, we are treated as if we had not broken God's law at all! Instead of being condemned for our sin, we are justified and counted as if we had been perfectly righteous all of our lives. We know we have all broken God's law and deserve his punishment. Justification is the work of God's mercy to save us from that punishment. In other words, God looks at us and sees the righteousness of Jesus instead of our sin.

We must be absolutely clear about where this righteousness comes from. Far too many people are counting on their good works to get them to heaven. Some would even say that the good works that they do *through the power of the Spirit* will get them to heaven. This may sound very convincing and biblical, but it is a FALSE GOSPEL. Justification does not come from God looking at *my* good works. Not even the good works that I have done through the new life I have in Christ. The only righteousness that God will accept is the righteousness of his Son. Justification is a gift of righteousness that is *given* to those *who have not earned it.*

❖ *Read Romans 3:23-24. According to verse 23, what have we all done?*

❖ *What word does Paul use do describe the freeness of our justification in verse 24?*

❖ *Romans 4:3-5 gives us a perfect example of how God made Abraham righteous. According to these verses, did Abraham's righteousness come from collecting good works?*

❖ *Where did his righteousness come from?*

Here we see that Abraham's righteousness did not come from himself. God simply *counted* him righteous because of his faith. Because of Christ's finished work on the cross, God will do the same thing for all who believe. "For by a single offering he has perfected for all time those who are being sanctified."[46]

---

[46] Hebrews 10:14

❖ *According to Paul's teaching in Romans 4:3-5, how is a person counted righteous (or justified)?*

❖ *According to Titus 3:7, how are we justified?*

Here we have two vital truths that relate to our salvation. We do have a responsibility to believe, but salvation is a work of the grace of God. This is the consistent testimony of Scripture. The tension between the two can tempt us to choose one truth over the other, but we dare not do that. To lose either of these would lead to great misunderstanding. We must understand that our salvation is from the grace of God alone so that we do not take any credit for it. On the other hand, we must understand that it is through faith in Christ so that we know how a person must respond to the gospel. Only those who repent of sin and trust in Christ are saved. This is our responsibility and if we do not believe, we cannot blame God, because we chose not to obey the gospel.

❖ *According to Titus 3:7, what is the result of being regenerated and justified?*

This is another reference to our great hope in Christ. According to the gospel, we are not only part of the kingdom, but we are heirs with Christ. This means that God has brought us into his family and allows us to share in the inheritance that belongs to Christ. The gospel is about allowing us, as sinful as we were, to share in Christ's own blessings and glory!

> The glory that you have given me I have given to them, that they may be one even as we are one, I in them and you in me, that they may become perfectly one, so that the world may know that you sent me and loved them even as you loved me. Father, I desire that they also, whom you have given me, may be with me where I am, to see my glory that you have given me because you loved me before the foundation of the world. (John 17:22-24)

❖ *Finally, what does Paul command Titus to do with this "sound doctrine" of the gospel in Titus 3:8?*

❖ *Why does Paul want him to insist so strongly on these things?*

This is the fourth time that Paul mentions good works, and there is still one more in Titus 3:14. The gospel and the good works that it produces in the believer are central themes in the book of Titus. Paul intentionally places good works after what

God has already done for us in the gospel. God has regenerated us and justified us so that we will do good works.

As we have already seen in this wonderful book, salvation is not only about the forgiveness of sins, but also about bringing glory to our saving God. He has saved us to be his special people in this dark and sinful world. Therefore, while we stand boldly against good works *for* salvation, good works are to be the defining mark of God's people. May our lives shine with good works that display the glory of the gospel of Jesus Christ.

> For by grace you have been saved through faith. And this is not your own doing; it is the gift of God, not a result of works, so that no one may boast. For we are his workmanship, created in Christ Jesus for good works, which God prepared beforehand, that we should walk in them. Ephesians 2:8-10

Chapter 11

Exercise Church Discipline

> [9]But avoid foolish controversies, genealogies, dissensions, and quarrels about the law, for they are unprofitable and worthless. [10]As for a person who stirs up division, after warning him once and then twice, have nothing more to do with him, [11]knowing that such a person is warped and sinful; he is self-condemned.
> Titus 1:9-11

Now we come to Paul's next instructions for Titus as he seeks to establish the churches on the island of Crete. Having so clearly established the nature and work of the gospel, he now warns Titus of the false doctrines that will arise to divide the body of Christ.

This chapter deals with many of the same truths that were covered in chapter 5, which is entitled "Boldly Oppose False Teaching." In that chapter, we learned that the elders must be sound in their faith and bold in confronting false teachers. The truth must be guarded as the foundation of everything else that is said or done in the church.

This chapter will go into further detail in dealing with false doctrine and sin, especially in the lives of the church members themselves. Certain truths will overlap with chapter 5, but this chapter will seek to address the following issues:

- What does the church do when the gospel is compromised by divisive teaching or disgraced by sinful living?
- What is the role of the church members in dealing with sin or false teaching?
- Why is this necessary and what will happen to the church if we do not do it?

The instructions we find in verses 9-11 teach what is commonly called church discipline. This refers to the corrective actions that a church must take when false teaching or sin creeps into a body of believers. Sadly, this is not an *if*, but a *when*. When these issues arise among the brethren, the church must know what to do. In these verses, we find the answer.

The Problem

The entire book of Titus has continually brought us back to one message – the gospel of Jesus Christ. In Titus 3:9, we find a transition from the sound doctrine to the poisoned doctrine.

❖ *What terms does Paul use to describe the false doctrine? (Titus 3:9)*

In this list of false teachings and dangers, we find a reference to the teachings that were mentioned in Titus chapter 1. It is not clear whether this was one group of false teachers or many groups; however, we can be certain that these teachings were not sound doctrine. As we have seen, these teachings were leading people away from the truth and into error and ungodly living.

Paul does not elaborate on these teachings for Titus, but simply tells him to avoid them at all costs.

So how can we know what the false teaching is if Paul does not explain it for us? The answer is simple. We are to be so well grounded in the truth that any time another alternative comes along, it stands out like a sore thumb. The emphasis in this letter is not on what everyone else is saying, but rather on what has God said. When that is clear, false doctrine does not stand a chance. "Hold the truth, my friends, and hold it as the easiest method of sweeping away heresies and false doctrines."[47]

This, however, could not be said for the church on the island of Crete. They were very weak and vulnerable to false teaching, as we have already noticed. The false teachers and their followers were already among them.

❖ *What does Titus 3:10 say these teachings will "stir up" in the church?*

As Paul has already shown, there is a direct connection between healthy teaching and healthy churches. Here Paul is obviously warning us not to let the preaching of the gospel and proper living be replaced by other things. These false teachings would catch people's attention and draw their minds and hearts away from the healthy doctrine that they needed.

---

[47] Spurgeon, C. (2007). *The New Park Street Pulpit Vol.1&2.* Grand Rapids, Michigan: Baker Books. Sermon 87 (p.275)

❖ *In 1 Timothy 1:3-5, Paul gives a very similar warning and points out the goal of all sound doctrine. What is the aim of sound doctrine according to verse 5?*

❖ *What do the other doctrines "promote," according to verse 4?*

This is absolutely essential. God is not interested in amazing us with mysteries and hidden secrets. He desires the transformation of the believer. This is what the entire book of Titus is about! In this book, Paul gives us the perfect model of sound teaching and the transformation that it produces.

The faithful church will keep this goal in mind. They will be faithful in preaching the truth so that they might also be faithful in living the truth. They will have a hunger for the Word and a longing to obey.

This aspect of faithfulness to the Word of God is the first element of church discipline. There is no better way to correct falsehood and error than to preach the Word. The issues that Paul is dealing with in these verses arise when false teaching begins to find a foothold among those who should know better. Paul warns that this *will* happen. In fact, this is exactly what he faced as he planted churches himself. There always seemed to be another group of teachers who were quick to come behind him and distort the gospel that he had preached. Listen to how Paul warns the elders of the church in Ephesus who he personally new and loved:

I know that after my departure fierce wolves will come in among you, not sparing the flock; and from among your own selves will arise men speaking twisted things, to draw away the disciples after them. Acts 20:29-30

Notice that Paul tells them that this will happen soon and that some of these very men would be involved. It is far too easy for us to assume that this danger is distant problem that would never affect those we know and love. These verses make it clear that the danger is always looming.

❖ *Look up 2 Timothy 3:12-13. What does Paul say about the danger of false teaching in the future? Will it get worse or will it go away eventually?*

Will these men look like false teachers?

❖ *2 Corinthians 11:13-15*

The Solution

❖ *What is the process that Paul lays out for dealing with these divisive teachings in Titus 3:10?*

1.

2.

3.

❖ *Look up Matthew 18:15-17 and notice how Jesus describes this process.*

1.

2.

3.

4.

In Titus, the issue is about doctrine and division. In Mathew 18, the issue is personal sin.

❖ *From these two passages, do we learn that false doctrine should be dealt with in the same way as sin or in a different way?*

In 1 Corinthians 5, we find the church in Corinth allowing a very sinful man to remain among them. Read the whole chapter and notice the following:

❖ *What is the proper attitude toward sin in the church? (v.2)*

Sin is often overlooked in the name of humility and love. Ignoring sin however, is not true humility or love. Instead, it reveals arrogance and pride on our part. How could we take sin lightly when God has prepared an eternal hell for the punishment of these sins? Have we forgotten the price that God paid to redeem us from sin and purify us to be his people? We must be a people who mourn over sin. This will also prevent a judgmental attitude toward the one who is in sin. If we are people who truly fear God and mourn over sin, we will not be able to overlook our own failures and weaknesses as we seek to help our brothers and sisters deal with their sin.

❖ *According to 1 Corinthians 5:2 and 5, what must be done?*

In this verse, we see the common theme of separation from the man who is hardened in sin. We must remember that this is not the way to deal with every sin. These instructions are only for those who have chosen to harden their hearts against every effort to restore them. This is only for the unrepentant who refuse to obey the clear teaching of the Scripture.

❖ *What is the twofold goal in verse 5?*

This verse is very instructive. It tells us that those who are put out of the church are delivered from the protection of the body of Christ and are turned back over to Satan. The goal is the destruction of the flesh. In other words, this person is under the judgment of God. How many churches have lost this concept completely? Church discipline is not an issue to take lightly.

In saying this, we must also notice that church discipline is done in love and in hope. Discipline is always intended to bring the person to repentance and salvation. It must never be done in self-righteousness or in a vengeful spirit, but in hope of the person's eternal salvation.

❖ *Who was to be involved – elders only, or the entire church? (1 Corinthians 5:4)*

❖ *By whose authority does Paul instruct them to deliver this man to Satan? (1 Corinthians 5:4)*

❖ *What is the effect of sin in the church, according to 1 Corinthians 5:6?*

This gets to the heart of the issue. Why must a church gather in the name of the Lord Jesus to put out the unrepentant man? It is a testimony to the incredibly destructive nature of sin. Sin spreads through the church as leaven does through bread, and this demands a complete removal of those who persist in known sin. If the church tolerates sin or false teaching, it will spread. The only way to keep leaven from spreading is to keep it out of the dough, and it is the same with sin. God's people must consistently deal with sin to keep it from doing damage. This means that believers must deal with the sin in their own lives on a daily basis, and any who live in unrepentant sin must be dealt with by separation.

Notice that Paul tells them to "cleanse out the old leaven so that you may be a new lump, as you are really unleavened." This simply means that the true church is a regenerated and justified group of people. They are pure in God's eyes. God sees them as they will be when they stand before him in heaven – unleavened by sin. The purging is to remove those who, though professing to believe in the Lord, are living in open defiance of him. The goal of this purging is to have local churches that actually live like believers.

❖ *What does Paul say this purging looks like in 1 Corinthians 5:11?*

This is the purging that we find in Titus 3:10. This separation from those who choose to live like the world is God's pattern throughout the Scriptures. This raises an important question in our dealings with those who are not believers. If we are to separate from those who claim to be believers and yet live like the world, how are we to deal with the world?

❖ *Does this apply to unbelievers as well, or only to believers? (1 Corinthians 5:9-13)*

This text teaches us that church discipline is a special responsibility of the church toward those who claim to be believers. The local church is to represent those who belong to Christ. Christ deals with those who are his sheep and church discipline is a part of how he does this. Christ will deal with the world on the Day of Judgment, but Christ always disciplines those who are his sheep so that they may share in his holiness.[48] We must remember that even this discipline is part of God's grace towards those who are his children. What we learn from Titus 3:10 and these other verses is that the local church has an important role to play in this grace towards the flock.

In our day of tolerance, we are taught that we cannot make judgments like this about other people. While there must be humility in dealing with situations like this, and while we do not want to make careless judgments that are not founded on truth, we also have a responsibility to judge biblically.

❖ *What does Paul tell Titus about the man who does not accept godly rebuke in Titus 3:11?*

Paul certainly did not have a problem with judging the tree by its fruit. Often, those who teach falsehood do not openly attack the truth, but simply begin to cast doubt on it as they call for more openness to "other ideas." While other opinions may be

---

[48] Hebrews 12:10 "He disciplines us for our good, that we may share his holiness."

tolerated in areas of conscience, such as Romans 14 describes[49], they cannot be tolerated in the area of our sound doctrine. The church must be clear in teaching that the gospel is a black and white issue. There is no gray area. While a diversion from sound doctrine can seem so harmless at times, it is a deadly error and Paul tells Titus to deal with it as such.

The Effect of Godly Discipline in the Church

Each of these instructions is essential to our understanding of proper church discipline. Many churches choose to overlook these inconvenient instructions, but they do so to their own harm. Let us take some time and notice some of the effects of this kind of church discipline.

First, it allows for real restoration and repentance. Remember the goal is not to put people out of the church, but to lovingly deal with sin. There is to be a simple confrontation at first, and the goal is to deal with the sin at that stage. It is only when stubbornness in sin becomes evident that the other levels have to come into play.

Man's wisdom may think it is offering mercy to an individual by not confronting sin, but nothing could be further from the truth. It is only when sin is confronted and these steps are lovingly applied that deeply rooted sin can be exposed and dealt with. In light of sin's effect on the entire church and the individual, this is the only loving thing to do.

---

[49] Romans 14:4-5 "Who are you to pass judgment on the servant of another? It is before his own master that he stands or falls. And he will be upheld, for the Lord is able to make him stand. One person esteems one day as better than another, while another esteems all days alike. Each one should be fully convinced in his own mind."

❖ We must pay attention to what 2 Thessalonians 3:13-15 says about putting a person out of the church. What is the attitude we are to have with those who are facing this discipline? (v.15)

❖ What does Paul tell the Corinthian believers to do with a repentant man who had been put out of the fellowship in 2 Corinthians 2:5-8?

Secondly, we see that this discipline produces a pure church that is waiting for her Bridegroom. In 1 Corinthians 5:6-8, Paul points back to the beautiful picture of the Passover night from the book of Exodus. On the night of the Passover, the children of Israel were to sacrifice a perfect lamb, put its blood on the door, and eat the lamb with unleavened bread as they waited for their deliverance (see Exodus 12:14-28[50]). This is a perfect picture of the

---

[50] Exodus 12:14-28 "This day shall be for you a memorial day, and you shall keep it as a feast to the LORD; throughout your generations, as a statute forever, you shall keep it as a feast. Seven days you shall eat unleavened bread. On the first day you shall remove leaven out of your houses, for if anyone eats what is leavened, from the first day until the seventh day, that person shall be cut off from Israel. On the first day you shall hold a holy assembly, and on the seventh day a holy assembly. No work shall be done on those days. But what everyone needs to eat, that alone may be prepared by you. And you shall observe the Feast of Unleavened Bread, for on this very day I brought your hosts out of the land of Egypt. Therefore you shall observe this day, throughout your generations, as a

gospel. As Paul says in 1 Corinthians 5:7, Christ was God's spotless lamb who was sacrificed. In the same way that the children of Israel put away leaven, the church is to put away the leaven of sin as we wait for our final deliverance when Christ returns.

We will close with the following quote by C.H. Spurgeon as he forcefully addresses those who say that the gospel of grace leads to unholy living:

> We challenge all those who love to speak against our doctrines to prove that there is a single one of them which has an unholy tendency. Charge us with not holding good works? Come and try to get into our church, and you will soon have a proof that you are wrong. Why, we would not have you, sir, if you would give us a thousand pounds, unless we considered you were a holy man. If you have not good works...and if you were to steal into our church, you

---

statute forever. In the first month, from the fourteenth day of the month at evening, you shall eat unleavened bread until the twenty-first day of the month at evening For seven days no leaven is to be found in your houses. If anyone eats what is leavened, that person will be cut off from the congregation of Israel, whether he is a sojourner or a native of the land. You shall eat nothing leavened; in all your dwelling places you shall eat unleavened bread." Then Moses called all the elders of Israel and said to them, "Go and select lambs for yourselves according to your clans, and kill the Passover lamb. Take a bunch of hyssop and dip it in the blood that is in the basin, and touch the lintel and the two doorposts with the blood that is in the basin. None of you shall go out of the door of his house until the morning. For the LORD will pass through to strike the Egyptians, and when he sees the blood on the lintel and on the two doorposts, the LORD will pass over the door and will not allow the destroyer to enter your houses to strike you. You shall observe this rite as a statute for you and for your sons forever. And when you come to the land that the LORD will give you, as he has promised, you shall keep this service. And when your children say to you, 'What do you mean by this service? you shall say, 'It is the sacrifice of the LORD's Passover, for he passed over the houses of the people of Israel in Egypt, when he struck the Egyptians but spared our houses.'" And the people bowed their heads and worshiped. Then the people of Israel went and did so; as the LORD had commanded Moses and Aaron, so they did."

would be turned out in a week, if you lived in sin and unrighteousness...and you would see whether we did not hold the necessity of good works. If you did not exhibit them every day we would cast you out from amongst us, and have no fellowship with the unfruitful works of darkness, but rather reprove them.[51]

> *You are the light of the world. A city set on a hill cannot be hidden.... In the same way, let your light shine before others, so that they may see your good works and give glory to your Father who is in heaven. Matthew 5:14&16*

---

[51] Charles Haddon Spurgeon (2009-08-19). Spurgeon's Sermons Volume 2: 1856 - Enhanced Version (Kindle Locations 4025-4031). Christian Classics Ethereal Library. Kindle Edition.

Chapter 12

The Body United

> [12]When I send Artemas or Tychicus to you, do your best to come to me at Nicopolis, for I have decided to spend the winter there. [13]Do your best to speed Zenas the lawyer and Apollos on their way; see that they lack nothing. [14]And let our people learn to devote themselves to good works, so as to help cases of urgent need, and not be unfruitful. [15]All who are with me send greetings to you. Greet those who love us in the faith. Grace be with you all. Titus3:12-15

In the previous chapter, we learned about the importance of purity in the body of Christ. This means that the Church is far more than a club or general gathering of people with common interests. The church of Jesus Christ is a connected body of believers who share in the life of God through the Holy Spirit. As we learned in chapter 7 of this study, we are purchased by the blood of Christ, so that we might be a "people for his own possession." This is why God's word demands church discipline in cases of unrepentant sin yet this truth also binds us together in a glorious unity. The fellowship of God's people is a glorious gift of our salvation.

❖ *Read John 17:22-23. What does Jesus share with us in verse 22?*

❖ *Why does Jesus share this glory with us according to verse 22?*

❖ *What is the effect of our unity with God and each other?*

Clearly, God has a grand purpose for the church. This purpose involves loving fellowship in the body of Christ. These closing verses in Titus reveal this truth in a profound way.

Here we find some final instructions for Titus as well as a salutation. As we study these last few verses, our goal is to understand Paul's instructions and the implications they have for a healthy church. Just as this salutation brings a fitting end to this great letter, it also highlights a common thread that runs through each of its three chapters. We will seek to understand what Paul is saying in these verses and then close with some practical application.

❖ *What are Paul's personal plans in verse 12?*

❖ *What instructions do we find for Titus in verse 13?*

Laboring Together

These verses are simply a personal note to Titus and they inform him of Paul's plans. In these instructions, we learn of Paul's plan to send faithful co-laborers to work with Titus, and of the needs that Zenas and Apollos would have as they traveled through this region. Many of Paul's letters end in a very similar fashion. In our day and time, we might not catch the full significance of these instructions, but they were of utmost importance in the days of the early church. As we have already seen, there was an abundance of false teachers infiltrating the church. In many of the Epistles, we find men who had been trusted leaders and co-workers, yet had now forsaken the faith in doctrine or practice. These instructions serve to give a stamp of approval to faithful servants of Christ and warn of those who had strayed from the truth.

❖ *What are Paul's instructions for the church in verse 14?*

❖ *According to verse 14, what would make a person unfruitful?*

This is the fifth time that good works are mentioned in the book of Titus. It is necessary to remember what Paul has been talking about as he gives this command. These good works are directly tied to the instruction to take care of Zenas and Apollos. As these godly men traveled their way, they would be in need and completely dependent upon the generosity of the church family. This is the type of "urgent need" that Paul refers to in verse 14. In our day and age, we can easily miss the serious nature of his command. To understand this command fully, let us take some time to study other apostolic instructions about our brothers and sisters in Christ.

First, we need to understand that there is spiritual connection between all genuine believers. That is why Christ has chosen to call the church his *Body*. How we live and work together reflects this unity to the world.

❖ *Look up 3 John 5-8. According to verse 8, why should we support faithful servants of Christ?*

Here we see that supporting faithful men makes us "fellow workers for the truth." When believers support each other in the work of the Lord, they are a living picture of Christ's body working together to accomplish his will. Each part has a different function, yet each part supports the others.

❖ *Now read 2 John 7-11. What does verse 9 say about those who do not abide in the teaching of Christ?*

❖ *What instructions do we have for those who do not bring the teaching of Christ?*

❖ *According to verse 11, why is it so important not to even greet this false teacher?*

The Lord teaches us that we share in the deeds of those whom we support and approve. If we bless and serve God's people, we share in the reward of God's people. However, if we bless or approve of those who teach falsehood, we share in their wicked works. Many believers do not understand this very serious issue. This is what Paul is referring to in Titus 3:14 as he talks about being fruitful in good works. These are not good works that earn us a place in heaven; they are good works that reflect that we belong to Christ and his people.

❖ *According to Titus 3:14, do all believers naturally do these good works without training?*

We must understand this point in order to keep these instructions in perspective. Believers are still in need of God's grace and the training that it brings. Godly leaders like Titus are simply tools that God uses to do this great work. This is why it is so important that we constantly encourage our brothers and sisters toward love and good works, just as we see Paul doing in this verse.

Notice what Paul tells the Galatian believers about good works:

❖ *According to Galatians 6:10, who are we to serve with good works?*

❖ *Is the emphasis to be on the world or on our fellow saints?*

While this verse makes it clear that we are to serve all people, we also see that the emphasis is on our brothers and sisters in Christ. The good works that Titus was commanded to teach were not a tool to attract the world as many believe. As Titus chapter 2 teaches, good works are to bring glory to God and the gospel message. Christians are not people pleasers, but servants. At times the world will appreciate the good that we do, and at other times they will persecute us. The reason that Paul instructs the church to emphasize service to the household of faith is found in the value that Christ places on his Bride. The love and fellowship that Christians share should be a bright and shining light in this dark world. The world should look with awe at the love that believers have for each other. According to Jesus in his High Priestly prayer, the unity and fellowship of believers is the best evidence for the truth of the gospel. [52]

While many churches talk about good works, many also have a wrong perspective. Unfortunately, many churches focus 90% of their energy and good works on the lost, simply as a means of attracting members into the church. This is not why we do good works. Good works are to be a reflection of God's love and character, not a public relations move.

The instruction to help men like Zenas and Apollos flows directly from this truth. However, just as it is important to serve alongside our faithful brothers and sisters in the faith, it is also important *not* to serve alongside those who bring false doctrine and ungodliness into the church. The true unity that Christ describes does not come through accepting false teaching and ungodly living. Rather, it comes through opposing these things as a unified body.

This truth explains so many of the personal instructions that we find at the end of the epistles. In these instructions, we find many commendations of faithful believers, along with a few warnings as well. It was important to know who was walking like a true believer and who was not. We must remember that this could be a life or death issue in light of the intense persecution that the church faced. However, even more importantly, it is always an eternal issue. If false gospels are allowed in the church, they will spread like leaven with damning effects.

---

[52] John 17:20-21 "I do not ask for these only, but also for those who will believe in me through word, that they may all be one, just as you, Father, are in me, and I in you, that they also may be in us, so that the world may believe that you have sent me."

A Common Bond

Now we come to Paul's final instruction for Titus. The instructions found in Titus 3:15 come in the context of church discipline discussed in verses 10-11 and the service to the faithful brother mentioned in verses 13-14.

❖ *What does Paul tell Titus in chapter 3 verse 15?*

This may sound like a simple, "tell all of my friends hi for me" statement, but that is not all that Paul is saying. While it *is* directed to those who Paul loves, it is also singling out those who were abiding in the faith. First, we must remember that this church was being severely damaged by false brethren and false teachers. Secondly, we must also remember the clear instructions to separate from those who were unrepentant. Finally, we must also remember the warning from 2 John, not even to give a greeting to those who were bringing a false gospel. Paul's greeting implies a serious distinction. This is for those who are recognized by the church as holding fast to their profession. They give good evidence to the fact that they are truly born again and walking in the faith. In fact, the phrase that Paul uses to describe them is one of the greatest evidences of their faithfulness.

❖ *How does Paul refer to those who should be greeted?*

❖ *Now compare that with what John 13:35 tells us.*

❖ *Read 1 John 1:1-3. Why did the apostles preach this message about Christ according to verse 3?*

The message of the apostles was the message of God.[53] To reject the apostolic message, was to reject the truth of God and the way of salvation itself.

❖ *Notice what the apostle John says in 2 John 1-2. What is the bond that unites the apostle and the "elect lady"?*

❖ *Who else shares in that affection?*

---

[53] 1 Thessalonians 2:13 "And we also thank God constantly for this, that when you received the word of God, which you heard from us, you accepted it not as the word of men but as what it really is, the word of God, which is at work in you believers."

❖ *Clearly, the truth is what binds believers together.*
What does John say about the truth in 2 John 2?

This could seem to paint a picture of perfection that seems unrealistic and unrealized in our day-to-day experience. Is this talking about some sort of sinless perfection where believers never hurt each other or sin? No! To get a better understanding of what Paul is referring to when he says to "greet those who love us in the faith," we will look at 2 Corinthians 7:6-12. In these verses, we find Paul addressing a church that had a bad history of sin and divisiveness. It seems that many in this church were beginning to listen to the teachers who were trying to discredit Paul and his work. This church was in serious danger of abandoning Paul for the new "super-apostles" that were now desiring their attention. Paul had rebuked them for their sin and had challenged them to put a certain man out of the church. With all of the sin and other struggles that this church had, one might expect Paul to write them off completely. As we pick up in these verses, Paul is discussing their response to him.

❖ *Read 2 Corinthians 7:6-12. What did Titus report about the Corinthians in verse 7?*

Notice that they mourned over their sin and had a zeal for Paul. He was rejoicing in the fact that they still recognized the truth of his calling and message because it was evidence of their steadfastness in the faith. In the same way, true believers are those who abide in the apostle's teachings as recorded in the Scripture. For example, when we read the book of Titus, we accept it as the Word of God and humbly seek to obey and apply what it says. If a person today claims to be a follower of Christ yet does not abide in the clear teaching of the Scriptures, he is in great danger.

❖ *What was their response to the letter that Paul had sent them according to verses 9-10?*

❖ *According to verse 12, what was revealed through this incident?*

Believers sin, sometimes horribly. This is a sad reality in this life, but it is not the only reality. In these verses, we see a struggling church that repented of its sin with godly grief. Here we learn that the unity and faithfulness of true believers can be severely tested and tried, but we also see the work of God's grace in their lives as they are restored through Paul's loving rebuke. When Paul says to greet those who love us in the faith, he is not talking about a self-righteous group in the church who believe themselves to be model Christians. He is talking about the strong and the weak, the rich and the poor, those soaring high in faith and those bowed down with godly grief over their sin. He is speaking to the truly repentant who walk in the light, confessing their sin and the truth of the gospel message. This is the true church of Jesus Christ. While words cannot fully express the love Christ has for the church, the Holy Spirit is continually revealing these truths to our hearts.[54] God's will is that we continue to delve deeper into his love for us so that we might reflect that love to others. This is what we see reflected in the closing verses of this remarkable letter. The church is a beautiful, although imperfect, reflection of God's holiness and love.

This truth brings us full circle. In chapter one, we looked at the Great Commission and the call to make disciples of all nations. A holy and unified church is both the result of the Great Commission and the way to carry it out. When the Great Commission is properly obeyed, the church will be holy and unified. Moreover, when the church is holy and unified, it will be making disciples.

As we seek to follow our Savior and carry out the mission to which he has called us, may we also keep our eyes on the source of our strength. Paul's closing words to Titus remind us what truly builds and sustains this great work of God: "Grace be with you all."

Now to him who is able to do far more abundantly than all that we ask or think, according to the power at work within us, to him be glory in the church and in Christ Jesus throughout all generations, forever and ever. Amen. Ephesians 3:20-21

---

[54] 1 Corinthians 2:9-10 "But, as it is written, "What no eye has seen, nor ear heard, nor the heart of man imagined, what God has prepared for those who love him"-- these things God has revealed to us through the Spirit."

Bibliography

Baxter, R. (2007). *The Reformed Pastor.* Carlisle, Pennsylvania: Banner of Truth Trust.

Bunyan, J. (2008). *The Works of John Bunyan, complet, including 58 books.* B&R Samizdat Express. Kindle edition.

Luther, M. (2006). *Concerning Christian Liberty.* Public Domain Books. Kindle Edition.

Marvin R. Vincent, D. (1904). *Vincent's Word Studies in the New Testament Part Four.* New York: Charles Scribner's Sons.

Owen, J. (1971). *The Holy Spirit.* Grand Rapids, MI: Sovereign Grace Publishers.

Robertson, A. T. (1930). *Word Pictures in the New Testament Vol.2.* Grand Rapids, Michigan: Baker House Books.

Ryle, J. C. (2010). *Holiness: Its Nature, Hindrances, Difficulties, and Roots .* Unknown, Kindle Edtion.

Spurgeon, C. (2007). *The New Park Street Pulpit Vol.1&2.* Grand Rapids, Michigan: Baker Books.

Spurgeon, C. (2012, April Wednesday). *Metropolitan Tabernacle Pulpit.* Retrieved from Spurgeon Archive: http://www.spurgeon.org/sermons/0581.htm

W.E. Vine, M. F. (1996). *Vine's Complete Expository Dictionary of Old and New Testament Words.* Nashville, Tennesse : Thomas Nelson.

Henry, Matthew (2010-11-07). Unabridged Matthew Henry's Commentary on the Whole Bible (best navigation)) OSNOVA. Kindle Edition.

www.ingramcontent.com/pod-product-compliance
Lightning Source LLC
Chambersburg PA
CBHW060929040426
42445CB00011B/857